MARKETING GREATEST HITS

A MASTERCLASS IN MODERN MARKETING IDEAS

KEVIN DUNCAN

A & C Black • London

First published in Great Britain 2010

A & C Black Publishers Ltd
36 Soho Square, London W1D 3QY
www.acblack.com

A CIP record for this book is available from the British Library.

ISBN: 978-1-4081-2639-4

This book is produced using paper that is made from wood grown in
managed, sustainable forests. It is natural, renewable and recyclable.
The logging and manufacturing processes conform to the
environmental regulations of the country of origin.

Design by Fiona Pike, Pike Design, Winchester
Cartoons by Gray Jolliffe
Typeset by Saxon Graphics Ltd, Derby
Printed in the United Kingdom by Cox & Wyman, Reading RG1 8EX

As always, my writing is dedicated to my girls:
Sarah, Rosanna and Shaunagh.

Acknowledgements

My heartfelt thanks to Gordon Wise for the introduction, and to Lisa Carden for helping it all along.

Cartoons by Gray Jolliffe.

For regular free updates and new material visit kevinduncan.typepad.com/greatest_hits or contact the author at:

kevinduncan@expertadvice.co.uk
expertadviceonline.com

To purchase the Apps of this book, or its sister title *Business Greatest Hits*, visit:

www.businessgreatesthits.com
www.marketinggreatesthits.com

CONTENTS

OVERVIEW

What's the book all about?

Welcome to the definitive compendium of everything you need to know from the best minds in modern marketing – abridged, condensed, and ready for immediate action. Modern marketing is a blur of jargon with thousands of books all purporting to hold the key to relentless success. The working reality is often very different, so here you will find everything distilled and summarised so that you can become an authority yourself.

As well as saving hundreds of hours of reading time, you will be able to grasp ideas with pithy accuracy, explain them authoritatively to colleagues and, crucially, avoid being hoodwinked by those who claim to understand a concept when in fact they have got the wrong end of the stick.

You need no longer be afraid of getting to the point quickly. Six short chapters draw together the most important ideas using some basic unifying principles such as:

- **Big theories are not necessarily complicated – this book makes sense of them for you.**

- Simple ideas always work – you can apply them immediately to your business.

- Broad and often misused concepts can be clarified and demystified.

- What is strategy? There is no mystery and plain language reveals all.

- Treat case studies with extreme caution. If they were that easy, everyone would be doing it.

- Marketing for big and small businesses – anyone can 'do marketing' if they are well guided.

- Make sense of all the jargon and buzz words.

At the back of the book, all 40 books are presented as one-minute summaries to give the reader an immediate feel for the subjects.

How is it organised?

I have corralled 40 of the most interesting books into six sections covering the big themes, marketing principles, branding, consumer behaviour, creativity, and personal organisation. If you want to get to grips with one of these areas in particular, then head straight to that section. If you prefer a more sequential approach, then work your way through from the beginning. Although marketing is never chronological, you will at least be able to absorb the most popular current concepts, take a view on marketing, branding and consumers, examine the vexed area of creativity and then decide how to get sufficiently organised to enact some of it.

The six sections

There's no such thing as right and wrong in marketing. It's all a matter of opinion. As a result, there are potentially only two ways to determine what the 'right' strategy is:

- **the most senior person in the room says so;**
- **the person writing the case history retrospectively decrees that it was, when in fact it was probably luck.**

In the spirit of the second point, I have used a healthy dose of my own opinion to decide which books make the cut to appear in the book. I have chosen them either because they are widely acknowledged to be seminal works, or because they represent a particular stance or counterpoint to the prevailing view. As such, they may not all be the *most* famous, but they will offer contrasting views so that you can be aware of all the angles in a particular debate. I will be delighted if you disagree with my selections because this will mean that you are already reading widely and forming your own opinions.

Long Tails and Pirates: the big themes

In Chapter 1 we will examine some of the big themes that have affected modern marketing. For years people only ever paid attention to how brand leaders worked, on the grounds that they were the most successful, so you could simply copy their behaviour and become successful yourself. That's all very well, but what if you don't have those resources and power? That's where Adam Morgan's *Eating the Big Fish* comes in. It was arguably the first book to propose how the also-rans, or challenger brands, should behave. We'll look at what he suggests.

Corporations are simply clusters of individuals, so how do you enact these findings when you have carefully identified what needs to be done? Morgan's follow up book, *The Pirate Inside,* explains precisely that. He identifies all sorts of personal behaviour that could make it a lot easier to effect corporate change.

We then move on to examine the idea that, far from wanting to be a market leader, in fact the pursuit of market domination is old hat. You can make huge profits from tiny increments, according to Chris Anderson in *The Long Tail.*

Having committed customers is another crucial area, which is why, in *Commitment-led Marketing* by Jan Hofmeyr and Butch Rice, we scrutinise why the customers you think are most committed to you may not be.

Having a superb company profile is the goal of many top marketers, but Public Relations doesn't work any more, or does it? We look at the ins and outs of this tricky debate by examining *Flat Earth News* by Nick Davies.

And lastly in Chapter 1, we ask the question: have we made it all too complicated? *In Search of the Obvious* by Jack Trout rather suggests that we have. So we draw together all the themes, disentangle and rebuild them to create a basis for moving on to the next chapter.

The end of marketing?

In Chapter 2 we grapple with the vexed question: what is marketing anyway? Using *Marketing Stripped Bare* by Patrick Forsyth, we strip away all the jargon and get down to the bare bones of this strange alchemy. Is it that complicated? Not really.

There has been much talk in associated literature about whether marketing as a discipline is dead, much of it generated by one Sergio Zyman, author of *The End of Marketing as We Know it*. Since you are reading this we can reasonably assume that there is some life in the subject yet, but the debate rumbles on. As early as 1999, efforts were being made to relaunch marketing in a new guise, so we examine the thinking of John Grant in *The New Marketing Manifesto* to see if it is still very much present but back in new clothes.

Advertising has been the whipping boy of the marketing world for some time – accused of being outmoded and superseded by more modern media. We examine whether the old model is still working with *Meatball Sundae* by Seth Godin, and then revisit this circular debate with a look at *The End of Advertising as We Know it* by our old friend Sergio Zyman.

Finally, there are many who claim that marketing is now all about the Internet, and very little else. One of the first gangs to do so was Levine, Locke, Searls, and Weinberger in *The Cluetrain Manifesto,* first published in 2000, so we examine their thinking and see what effect it has had over the subsequent decade.

Lovemarks and Buzz: brands and branding

In Chapter 3 we are chasing another Holy Grail and trying to answer the elusive question: what is branding? This can be a bit like categorising snowflakes, so we begin with a thought-provoking look at *The Philosophy of Branding* with Thom Braun.

Then we get into the detail of how your brand should behave, looking at *Brand Manners* with Pringle and Gordon. You are going to have a brand image whether you like it or not, so you might as well *Manage Your Reputation*. We'll take some important advice from Roger Haywood.

Can you create a buzz around your brand and, if so, how do you do it? We examine the role of Public Relations and word of mouth with Salzman, Matathia and O'Reilly, in their book *Buzz*.

Can you engender loyalty beyond reason? This is a question posed and apparently answered by Saatchi & Saatchi. Brands that transcend the normal properties of trademarks become *Lovemarks*, according to their worldwide chief Kevin Roberts. We look at the implications.

And finally for this chapter, there is a school of thought that those involved with brands need to stop being control freaks and let consumers have a far greater influence on what brands are, so we rifle through a series of new ways to allow your brand to do this with John Grant in *The Brand Innovation Manifesto*, seven years after his effort in the previous chapter.

Affluenza, Herds and Quirkology: mysterious consumer behaviour

Chapter 4 looks at the mysterious world of consumer behaviour. Why do people do what they do, and what bearing, if any, can marketing have on their actions? People do some very strange things, as explained by Richard Wiseman in his book *Quirkology*. They panic when they are told to, particularly about things they do not understand (*Panicology*, Briscoe and Aldersey-Williams), and, in Western society at any rate, they always buy far more than they really need. This may be good for marketers but less so for the purchasers. We study *Affluenza* by Oliver James and *Enough* by John Naish to see what we can learn.

Are we all individuals, or do we simply copy each other all the time? Mark Earls, author of *Herd*, believes the latter – an idea explored further in *The Wisdom of Crowds* by James

Surowiecki, who argues that the collected view of groups is usually more accurate than that of one supposed expert.

We finish the chapter by looking at two related concepts from the highly popular Malcolm Gladwell. In *Blink*, he asserts that people are usually right if they trust their instincts – something marketers could learn from as they labour over mountains of data and research. In *The Tipping Point*, he shows that small things can make a big difference, thereby somewhat puncturing the bubble of those marketers who are always looking for the next big thing, the big idea or pushing for a larger budget. None of these may be necessary for success.

Creativity: can you learn it?

By Chapter 5 we are grappling with the tricky area of creativity. Can you learn it if you do not believe that you are naturally creative? We are all born to play and create, according to Pat Kane in *The Play Ethic,* and he should know because he also sings in the band *Hue And Cry.*

That's fine, but creativity is pointless without a purpose, argues Mark Earls in *Welcome to the Creative Age.* This is a fair counterpoint, since one of the greatest criticisms of the communications industry is random creativity for the sake of it, with little commercial result.

One way to embrace creativity is to try to emulate creative companies, so we look at that possibility with Fallon and Senn in *Juicing the Orange,* and with Barnes and Richardson in *Marketing Judo.*

This may all be a bit more complex than it looks. You can try applying some universal rules such as *The 22 Irrefutable Laws of Advertising* by Michael Newman, or you can try a range of techniques to stimulate creative ideas, which we look at with John Adair's *The Art Of Creative Thinking and* Pease and Lotherington's *Flicking your Creative Switch*.

Finally, modern thinking suggests that you can try to create something by involving lots of people, in what is often called co-creation. The classic example of this is *We-Think*, by Charles Leadbeater, who effectively wrote a best-selling book by getting 257 other people to help him write it on the Internet.

Personal organisation: how to get on with it

In the last chapter we concentrate on how on earth you can get all this thinking applied to your business. Keep it simple, says John Maeda in *The Laws of Simplicity*. Articulate yourself well, says Richard Heller in *High Impact Speeches*.

Presenting your company or brand well is crucial. We look at the art of pitching and presenting an argument with *How Not to Come Second* by David Kean, and *Perfect Pitch* by Jon Steel.

If you have trouble getting on with something, there is always the possibility that you are not the right person to do it. There is a knack to working this out that is well articulated by Michael E. Gerber in *The E-Myth Revisited*.

But really what it all boils down to is that you need a system to get anything done at all, says Fergus O'Connell in *Simply Brilliant*. Things either are or they aren't, so stop making excuses and get on with it. Sound advice indeed. Let's get on with the book then.

And finally...

Although the points in the books are often contradictory, we draw all the one-sentence summaries together to form an intriguing new marketing manifesto to inspire your approach.

"Casual Friday does not entitle you to call me 'Tel'."

CHAPTER 1.
LONG TAILS AND
PIRATES: THE BIG
THEMES

What do you do if you are not the brand leader?

Eating the Big Fish ADAM MORGAN

For years people only ever paid attention to how brand leaders worked, on the grounds that they were the most successful, so you could simply copy their behaviour and become successful yourself. That's all very well, but the logic is flawed for two reasons. First, if everyone could simply copy the principles of a successful brand leader, then they would all be brand leaders, which is impossible. Secondly, what if you don't have those resources or that power? You would have to do more with less. That's where Adam Morgan's *Eating the Big Fish* comes in. It was arguably the first book to propose how the also-rans, or challenger brands, should behave.

The book was first published in 1999 and recently reissued in a tenth anniversary edition. Its fundamental point is that most marketing books are written about brand leaders, but most marketing people don't work on leading brands, and so cannot apply the wisdom they contain. Challenger brands (that's everybody who isn't a brand leader) need to behave differently if they are to compete with the big boys – effectively doing more with less resource.

He proposes eight credos that might help:

1. **Break with your immediate past**
   Forget everything you think you know and think again.
   Far too many companies keep referring back to the
   past. This does not create the right attitude or
   preparation for a truly distinctive strategy.

2. **Build a lighthouse identity**

   State what you are insistently and emotionally – don't just reflect what consumers say they want, or base your approach on echoes of what your competition does.

3. **Assume thought leadership of the category**

   Become the one everyone talks about. If you haven't got the funds to swamp an audience with your message, then come up with an inspiring idea that they will all talk about.

4. **Create symbols of re-evaluation**

   Do the unexpected to get noticed. A change in company attitude can be conveyed rapidly by appearing in unusual places and saying unusual things.

5. **Sacrifice**

   Work out what you are *not* going to do. The ability to enact such a strategy relies on disciplined behaviour. Companies always want to be seen to be doing lots of things, when in fact doing one thing well could be more effective.

6. **Over-commit**

   Karate experts aim two feet below the brick to break it. It takes more effort than they really need but it guarantees the job gets done. This is the attitude that challenger brands require when enacting their marketing. Half-hearted attempts don't work, especially when you lack brand leader resources.

7. **Use advertising/publicity to enter popular culture**

   Playing by the existing rules in your sector or category won't work. You need to attach your brand to something that resonates in popular culture and make it stick.

8. **Become ideas-centred, not consumer-centred**
Constantly re-invent what you are doing. Successful challenger brands are not static, so you cannot invent something clever and rest on your laurels. Keep coming up with ideas and enacting them.

The one-sentence summary
Ignore what you have done before, decide on something distinctive to do, and do that one thing with full commitment.

This advice is helpful because it concentrates on the practical things that pretty much any marketer can do. Most of the credos can be used to overcome company inertia and get things underway. It can certainly help small, under-resourced marketing teams to mobilise a single idea, if they can be clear enough about what that one thing is. One of the great temptations in marketing is to do too much. As the old joke goes:

**Q. What does a Marketing Director do when a
    campaign doesn't work?**
A. Another campaign.

Brand leaders can also benefit from thinking like a challenger to stay number one – the Avis *'We try harder'* principle. If you have trouble persuading colleagues of the value of this approach, the book tells you how to run a workshop and apply all the thinking.

If there is one pitfall, it is that it is far too easy for people to grab the gist of the argument and then walk the corridors talking about *'building a lighthouse identity'* or *'sacrifice and over-commit',* without actually realising what they are saying and without the actions to follow it up (we will look at this in the next section).

Corporations are made up of people. How are you supposed to behave exactly?

The Pirate Inside ADAM MORGAN

Eating the Big Fish suggested how corporations should behave in order to be more competitive, but by 2004 Adam Morgan was developing another related theme. Corporations are simply clusters of individuals, so how do you enact these findings when you have carefully identified what needs to be done? His follow up book, *The Pirate Inside,* explains precisely this – he identifies all sorts of personal behaviour that could make it a lot easier to effect corporate change.

This is an issue that top management has been grappling with forever. The Chief Executive has just decreed that the company will now behave in a certain way, but how on earth does he or she make sure that employees actually do it? It's a problem worse than herding cats, and many good people and companies have gone to the wall trying.

The book suggests that powerful brands are built by people, not by proprietary methodologies. So the real issue is not so much the strategy, but how people need to *behave* when an organisation's systems seem more geared to slowing and diluting, rather than spurring and galvanising. In short, employees need permission to get on with change or, at the very least, they need to be given clever approaches to behaving differently so that they can make things happen.

To achieve this, Morgan says that you need to be a *Constructive Pirate.* This is not the same as anarchy where there are 'no rules', but requires a different *set* of rules. He explains nine ways of behaving that stimulate challenger brand cultures:

1. **Outlooking**
   Looking for different kinds of insights using a range of techniques including:
   * *emotional insertion* – putting a new kind of emotion into the category;
   * *overlay* – overlaying the rules of a different category on to your own;
   * *brand neighbourhoods* – radically re-framing your competitive set;
   * *grip* – finding a place for the brand to gain traction in contemporary culture.

2. **Pushing**
   Pushing ideas well beyond the norm. An idea that is only good enough and on-brief may not be enough.

3. **Projecting**
   Being consistent across far more media than the usual is essential.

4. **Wrapping**
   Communicating less conventionally with customers via customs, rituals and iconography that go much deeper than any overarching campaign theme.

5. **Denting**
   Respecting colleagues whilst making a real difference. Good *Denters* treat the answer 'no' as a request for further information.

6. **Binding**
   Having a contract that ensures everyone comes up

with the idea is important. This is a common purpose that makes teams get on with delivering it.

7. Leaning
Pushing harder for sustained commitment, or leaning into it, is a necessary piece of personal exposure. Faint-hearted approaches are less successful.

8. Refusing
Having the passion to say no. For example, refusing to accept that a particular issue cannot be overcome.

9. Taking it personally
A different professionalism that transcends corporate man, this type of taking it personally means that projects and ideas are pushed further by those involved in them.

The one-sentence summary
To make corporations change effectively, the people who work in them have to behave differently, or be told how to do so.

Even in big organisations, you need challenger sub-cultures to create the sort of energy and forward motion that is more common in smaller operations. The book shows you how to write your own 'articles' in your organisation. These are the new rules that encourage change to happen.

The Three Buckets is a good exercise whereby you have to categorise all your existing projects into *Brilliant Basics, Compelling Difference* and *Changing the Game* – usually with poignant results. If you only have initiatives in the first box, then no major change will occur.

Biting the Other Generals is a good concept based on an anecdote from the Seven Years War. A brilliantly unconventional General, James Wolfe, proved himself one of the most talented military leaders under King George III. When some of Wolfe's detractors tried to undermine him by complaining that he was mad, the king replied: *'Oh, he is mad, is he? Then I would he would bite some other of my generals.'* Morgan believes that good *Pirate* behaviour should be infectious and beneficial.

Market domination is old hat. You can make huge profits from tiny increments

The Long Tail CHRIS ANDERSON

Wanting to be a market leader is all very well, but there are those who believe that the pursuit of market domination is old hat. Endless choice is creating unlimited demand and you can make huge profits from tiny increments, according to Chris Anderson in *The Long Tail*. In 2006 he claimed that traditional business models attest that high-selling hits are required for success. These are at the high-volume end of a conventional demand curve.

But in the Internet era, the combined value of the millions of items that only sell in small quantities can equal or even exceed the best sellers. This is the now much-coveted long tail.

Modest sellers and niche products are now becoming an immensely powerful cumulative force. In this respect, many 'mass' markets are turning into millions of aggregated niches. You no longer need huge warehouses, retail outlets, or big inventory. Many products can be delivered online or on demand without any of these costly overheads.

The nine big rules of *The Long Tail* are:

1. **Move inventory way in...or way out**
   Either make your products available from the central warehouse and bypass the retail network, or outsource their storage in the same way that Amazon does.

2. **Let customers do the work**
   Customers will happily do for free what companies often spend millions on – reviewing and sifting the relative merits of products. This so-called 'crowdsourcing' tells you all you need to know about market demand.

3. **One distribution method doesn't fit all**
   Make your products available in as many channels as possible that are viable. The best *Long Tail* markets transcend time and space.

4. **One product doesn't fit all**
   If possible, divide your products into 'microchunks' so that customers can customise them for themselves, without you going to the heavy cost of doing so.

5. **One price doesn't fit all**
   One of the best understood principles of microeconomics is the power of elastic pricing. Different people will pay different prices for a variety of reasons. This maximises the value of your products and the size of the market.

6. **Share information**
   Information about buying patterns, when transformed into recommendations, can be a powerful marketing tool. Think Amazon.

7. Think 'and', not 'or'

Thinking that everything is an either/or choice is a mistake. The more abundant the storage and distribution system, the less discriminating you have to be in how you use it. It is worth noting that this is not a new concept – it was originally raised by Collins and Porras in *Built to Last* in 1994.

8. Trust the market to do your job

In abundant markets you can throw it all out there and see what happens, letting the market sort it out. Online markets in particular are highly efficient measures of the wisdom of crowds (see Chapter 4).

9. Understand the power of free

Because their costs are often near zero, digital markets can get as close to free as anyone can. In this respect, 'free' doesn't have to evoke visions of piracy or the evaporation of value.

The one-sentence summary

Endless choice is creating unlimited demand so you probably need to re-think your business model: make everything available and help customers find it easily (online).

All of this can be summarised as: lower your costs, think niche and lose control to the market. This is a very original and thought-provoking book. It takes a while to get into, but it's worth it. It introduces reasonably complicated mathematical theory in a user-friendly way, particularly micro-analysis of the very end of what is a very Long Tail.

This is where helpful truths about the economics of your market can be seen properly.

Contemporary examples from music, books and films lend a populist slant to the theory, which should appeal widely. Meanwhile, old theories such as the 80/20 rule receive a thorough going-over. The author points out that it's never exactly 80/20, that the percentages can apply to different things (products, sales or profits) and that they don't necessarily add up to 100 either.

The Long Tail model works best with true Internet and digital products that do not take up any storage space. For example, Amazon books still require storage space that has a certain cost, even allowing for a high proportion of approved sellers. iTunes, however, does not. So careful thought is required as to the nature of the market you are analysing, and whether the observations can find useful application to your product.

Why the customers you think are most committed may not be

Commitment-led Marketing HOFMEYR & RICE

In 2000, a book came out with a rather unremarkable title, but a fairly remarkable finding. *Commitment-led Marketing*, subtitled *The key to brand profits is in the customer's mind*, discovered that some customers appear to be loyal because they habitually buy a product, but this does not mean to say that they are committed to it. When a new player comes into the market offering a suitable alternative, they could actually be the first to defect. If the majority of the marketing world had read this, they would have been running to their market share figures and panicking, because having committed customers is hallowed ground for all brand custodians.

The findings go something like this. Customer satisfaction is a poor predictor of behaviour – commitment is better. Loyalty is what customers have, and commitment is what they feel. This means that your research information can be highly misleading, because customers can appear deceptively loyal but actually be uncommitted. They might only use your brand because everyone else does (such as with the ubiquitous Microsoft), through lack of choice, affordability, distribution, or a range of other factors. Given half a chance, they might move to a competitor straightaway.

As such, the key to brand profits lies in the customer's mind. The conversion model in the book allows you to segment users by commitment to stay, and non-users by openness to adopt your brand. By applying this to your brand and to your competitors, you can identify the right strategy to defend market share (if you are a large brand), or steal it (if small).

There is a useful segmentation element to the model. Users are entrenched or average (committed); shallow or convertible (uncommitted). Non-users are available or ambivalent (open); weakly or strongly (unavailable). Few clients correctly measure these features for all the brands in their market – if they did, they could make better informed decisions. The idea that 'satisfied' customers may be very prepared to leave your brand immediately is both clever and alarming. Are you measuring the wrong attribute? Can you identify a competitor's Achilles heel?

Even more frightening, a 'last straw' can make a committed user snap and switch to another brand. The moment is hard to predict, the decision is usually irreversible, and to cap it all they tend to become a missionary *against* your brand. That's a scary thought for marketers the world over.

The one-sentence summary
The customers that your data says are your most satisfied may be the most likely to leave tomorrow, so are you asking the right questions and measuring the right dimensions?

The book also contains a level-headed review of the most common mistakes that marketers make. They are:

1. **Unnecessary price-cutting**
   It erodes the total brand equity in the market and seldom results in long-term share increases.

2. **Unnecessary new product development**
   Ignoring commitment to existing brands overestimates the success of new ones.

3. **Too much advertising**
   Advertising for small brands is less effective than for large.

4. **Too little advertising**
   A brand leader should behave like one.

5. **Inadequate management at point of purchase**
   Uncommitted users do not go out of their way to find brands.

6. **Believing that advertising can change perceptions**
   Advertising works best at reinforcing current beliefs.

7. **Spending according to value instead of commitment**
   Relationship managers are wrong to lavish attention just on high-value customers who are already very committed.

8. Spending too much on customers who are unavailable
Resistant potential customers would have to move from strongly to weakly unavailable to ambivalent to available. This road can be too long and unrealistic.

9. Trying to have a relationship with customers who don't want one
Lots of customers simply don't want relationships with your brand, so they shouldn't be forced to.

The problem with most database models is that they only use hard data. Adding commitment significantly enhances their value, and integrating behavioural and commitment measures with lifetime value enables the best decisions. The technology now exists to do this easily.

Wastage in direct marketing can now be reduced hugely because it is relatively easy to identify those who are not interested in your product, but it is important to realise that if a customer has a low value to the brand it does not mean they have a low value to the category. Do not make the mistake of automatically discarding all low-value customers.

The authors argue that using commitment in databases allows customised communication strategies, allowing marketers to vary tone, content and weight to increase profitability. In order to benefit from this thinking you would have to endorse the philosophy completely, invest heavily in implementing what it proposes, and be very patient whilst the data become apparent.

PR doesn't work any more, or does it?

Flat Earth News NICK DAVIES

Having a superb company profile is the goal of many top marketers, but Public Relations (PR) doesn't work any more. Or does it? Nick Davies waded in to this tricky debate in 2008 with his controversial book *Flat Earth News*. A journalist who started investigating his own colleagues, his industry-shocking accusations included:

1. **Global media is full of falsehood, distortion and propaganda**
   The whole system is rotten, he claims. It is merely collusion between the press and the PR agencies.

2. **The business of reporting the truth has been slowly subverted by the mass production of ignorance**
   Many stories are little more than loaded propaganda or near-fiction.

3. **Many stories are no more accurate than claiming the earth is flat**
   The Millennium Bug and Weapons of Mass Destruction in Iraq are classic examples. These have the power to taint government policy and pervert popular belief.

4. **Most reporters do not have time to check what they are sent**
   Instead they rely on the Press Association or PR stories to generate 'churnalism', a strand of journalism that verifies very little and merely recycles material from other sources.

His research shows that 70 per cent of stories are wholly or partly rewritten from wire copy, without further corroboration. With the help of researchers from Cardiff University, who ran a very detailed analysis of the contents and sources for the nation's daily news, he found that most reporters, most of the time, are not allowed to dig up stories or check their facts. This is because they are under intense pressure to release stories immediately, usually on the Internet. Once we realise this, he suggests, we effectively have a new model for understanding news.

The one-sentence summary
Most news stories are planted by PR agencies without verification and cannot be believed – everybody knows this, so the whole system is discredited.

This is a very ballsy, well-researched book, as you would expect from an investigative journalist. Revisiting the cosy relationship between PR and the media caused a significant stir, with PR agencies and newspapers up in arms about it. Had it been a broad-based polemic, railing against the system generally, it might have been less remarkable. However, it named names, in a specific and authoritative way, and although there is a tinge of 'chip on shoulder' about it, neither industry really had any decent answers to the allegations. *'Finally I was forced to admit that I work in a corrupted profession,'* he claimed.

This whistle-blowing broke Fleet Street's unwritten rule because he also investigated his own colleagues. Working with a network of off-the-record sources, he uncovered a series of damning stories, including:

1. **The prestigious Sunday newspaper which allowed the CIA and MI6 to plant fiction in its columns.**

2. **The daily newsroom where senior reporters casually refer to 'nig nogs', and where executives routinely reject stories about black people.**

3. **The respected quality paper that was so desperate for scoops that it hired a conman to set up a front company to entrap senior political figures.**

4. **More than one paper that supports law and order while simultaneously paying cash bribes to bent detectives and hiring private investigators to steal information.**

He also examines the parameters set by the media moguls and outlines the rules of production that they dictate:

1. **Cut costs by running cheap stories**
   This involves selecting safe facts and ideas, and making them sound more remarkable than they truly are.

2. **Avoid the electric fence**
   These are the regulatory bodies that can hurt the press, who must never be crossed to the point where they impinge on the way the papers operate. They can usually be appeased by always giving both sides of the story.

3. **Increase revenue by giving the readers what they want to believe in**
   The more nonsense they lap up, the more you give them. This has little to do with breaking genuinely new information that may be in the public interest.

We will return to other aspects of the PR debate in later chapters. This book represents one extreme. As a layperson, you might find it rather alarming. As a marketer who wishes to deploy PR, the fact that many stories apparently run pretty much unchallenged when they are fed in by agencies could mean that PR has greater influence over editorial policy than ever before. But if it is running in media that are discredited, does it retain its potency?

Have we made it all too complicated?

In Search of the Obvious JACK TROUT

And finally for this chapter, we ask the question: have we made it all too complicated? *In Search of the Obvious* by Jack Trout, published in 2008, rather suggests that we have. Subtitled *The Antidote for Today's Marketing Mess,* this is a pointed polemic about the state that marketing has got itself into – or should that be, into which it has got itself? He gives marketing, advertising, research, Wall Street, the Internet, and several named companies a thorough pasting.

In his opinion, instead of concentrating on segmentation, customer retention, search engine optimisation, and scores of other over-complex techniques, marketers should be looking for that simple, obvious and differentiating idea. Particular culprits here are people and organisations that deliberately put complication in the way of the obvious – and shoot themselves in the foot as a result. He also believes that because many people fear the activity of thinking, they simply follow suggestions made by others to avoid having to think for themselves.

The main points are:

1. **We seem to have no time to think any more**
   Many meetings are little more than gadget envy sessions. If you really want to solve a problem, try some of the angular thinking techniques in the next list.

2. **Marketing people overcomplicate everything**
   'The art of being wise is the art of knowing what to overlook.' William James

3. **Mission statements are bunk**
   A survey of 300 mission statements revealed that the words used in them are all the same: the most common were service (230 mentions), customers (211), quality (194), value, employees, growth, environment, profit, leader and best.

4. **Sales, technology and performance leadership are all valid concepts**
   Thought leadership is not – it doesn't mean anything (compare this with Adam Morgan's stance at the beginning of this chapter).

5. **The marketing world is full of blunders these days**
   The biggest culprits are: 'me too' products or ideas, being unclear what you are selling, untruthful claims, and arrogance brought on by success.

The one-sentence summary
Marketing is a mess, so stop overcomplicating everything and do some simple thinking based on your brand's obvious differentiating characteristics.

Some helpful thinking techniques based on the obvious:

- *Substitute* – what could you substitute in the approach, materials, ingredients or appearance?

- *Combine* – what could you blend with an existing idea?

- *Adapt* – what else is this idea like? What could you copy?

- *Magnify or minimise* – what if you added, lengthened, strengthened or subtracted?

- *Put it to other uses* – in what other ways could you use what you already have?

- *Eliminate* – what could you get rid of?

- *Reverse or rearrange* – what could you transpose or look at backwards?

- *Shift audiences* – is there a segment being ignored to whom you can pitch your product?

His main targets for criticism are:

- advertisers who look for the creative and edgy, not the obvious;

- marketing people who get hopelessly entangled in corporate egos and complicated projects;

- research people for generating more confusion than clarity;

- big companies for their ill-fated marketing programmes or lack of proper strategy;

- **Wall Street for putting too much emphasis on growth that is unnecessary and can actually be destructive to brands.**

Trout believes that the search for any marketing strategy is the search for the obvious. We are in an era of pervasive competition. Category after category is perceived as a commodity. This is the central reason that the critically important function of marketing is in such a mess. It's also why the average Chief Marketing Officer barely lasts beyond two years in the job.

Marketers should be searching for that simple, obvious and differentiating idea. This search should begin with what Trout considers the best book ever written on marketing – even though it was published in 1916 and isn't about marketing. Entitled *Obvious Adams: The Story of a Successful Business Man,* it lays out the five tests of an obvious idea that will lead you to the right marketing strategy for any product.

The fundamental problem is that effective marketing is both complicated and extremely simple – so simple that professional marketers overlook the most obvious and effective ideas entirely, in an attempt to be clever or creative. But if an idea is obvious to you, it will be obvious to your customers, which is why it will work.

CHAPTER 1 WISDOM

- Ignore what you have done before, decide on something distinctive to do, and do that one thing with full commitment.

- To make corporations change effectively, the people who work in them have to behave differently, or be told how to do so.

- Endless choice is creating unlimited demand so you probably need to re-think your business model: make everything available and help customers find it easily (online).

- The customers that your data says are your most satisfied may be the most likely to leave tomorrow – are you asking the right questions and measuring the right dimensions?

- Most news stories are planted by PR agencies without verification and cannot be believed – everybody knows this, so the whole system is discredited.

- Marketing is a mess, so stop overcomplicating everything and do some simple thinking based on your brand's obvious differentiating characteristics.

"Give me a double shot of anything –
Since marketing died I have no idea."

CHAPTER 2.
THE END OF
MARKETING?

What is marketing anyway?

Marketing Stripped Bare PATRICK FORSYTH

So now we grapple with the vexed question: what is marketing anyway? Can it really be that complicated? Not really, says Patrick Forsyth, whose book *Marketing Stripped Bare* was originally published as *Everything You Need to Know About Marketing* in 1990. Twenty years later, it still allows the reader to strip away all the jargon and get down to the bare bones of this strange alchemy. Billed as an insider's guide to the secret rules of marketing, it covers everything from advertising and PR through to sales, distribution, and electronic media. The overall message is that marketing is central to every company, but it doesn't have to be wrapped up in complicated jargon so that everyone gets confused.

First principles are:

- **marketing acts as a bridge between an organisation and the outside world, its markets and customers;**

- **marketers should remember that all the other departments think they are important too;**

- **the basic shape of the marketing plan, the promotion mix, selling and distribution remain the same for pretty much every company.**

It then sets about giving the reader easy ways to write marketing plans, examine the promotional mix and organise research methodology, even if they have never officially been trained in these areas. As such it could be perfect as an educational tool for anyone entering the discipline for the first time.

It is also full of interesting quotes to help inspire good presentations and more original work:

1. **Opportunities are usually disguised as hard work, so most people do not recognise them**
   Opportunities don't simply appear. They become apparent after careful analysis of good information, and some smart thinking.

2. **Pessimists make poor planners**
   Marketing requires a dash of optimism – not so much as to be irritatingly gung-ho, but enough to see the positive in possibilities and pursue them until proven unfruitful.

3. **There is only one thing in the world worse than being talked about, and that is not being talked about**
   Notoriety is the objective of most marketing, albeit you are after a good image rather than a bad one. Being totally unknown doesn't get your brand anywhere.

4. **If you call a spade a spade, you won't last long in the advertising business**
   Lying is clearly not acceptable, but you do at least have to have some flair for turning the mundane into something more appealing.

5. **An idea that is not dangerous is unworthy of being called an idea at all**
   Many so-called ideas don't deserve to be described as such. A true idea requires an element of uncertainty if it is to have any merit.

6. **If at first an idea isn't totally absurd, there's no hope for it**
   Pushing even further, if an idea doesn't make you feel uncomfortable, it's probably no good. Analyse your marketing ideas using this criterion.

7. **My interest is in the future because I am going to spend the rest of my life there**
   Everything changes and nothing stays the same. Marketing thrives on movement. So make sure that you are prepared to change your mind regularly, and constantly reinvent.

All of these can be used as interesting starting points for ingenious marketing. The rough rule of thumb is that if anything makes you feel really comfortable, it is probably quite dull and so needs reassessing.

The one-sentence summary

Marketing acts as a bridge between an organisation and the outside world, and is central to every company, but it doesn't have to be wrapped up in complicated jargon that confuses everyone.

Although the book could be regarded as quite simplistic if taken literally, it is written in a very amusing way that whisks the reader swiftly from one principle to another with the minimum of fuss. At face value, the book is a body of information rather than opinion, but nevertheless it does have angles lurking within. If you take anything from it and repeat it directly to a colleague, you may be accused either of being cynical, or too simplistic. In truth, everything should be made as simple as possible, but no simpler. Do not be tempted to wrap up clear, original thinking in impenetrable jargon, but do allow ideas to shine in interesting ways.

They think it's all over...it is now

The End of Marketing as We Know it SERGIO ZYMAN

There has been much talk in associated literature about whether marketing as a discipline is actually dead, much of it generated by one Sergio Zyman, author of *The End of Marketing as We Know it,* first published in 2000. I don't think we'll panic quite yet. The very fact that you are reading this book suggests that there is still some life in the subject, but the debate certainly rumbles on, as this chapter shows. His opening salvo launches with six big points:

1. **Marketing today is all about image, but it isn't working properly.**

2. **Marketing is a science, not an art.**

3. **Marketing is too important to be left to the marketing department.**

4. **Marketers must be accountable to shareholders.**

5. **Focus on results, not activities.**

6. **Megabrands are a rotten idea.**

The last one is fairly extraordinary given that the author is the former Chief Marketing Officer of Coca-Cola. He then sets about defining the Principles of New Marketing. There are too many to list in full, but the main ones are:

1. **The sole purpose of marketing**
   ...is to sell more to more people, more often, and at higher prices.

2. **Marketing is serious business**
   ...and increasingly serious business is about marketing.

3. **Marketing is not magic**
   ...and marketers do themselves no favours when they pretend that it is.

4. **Marketing is a professional discipline**
   You can't leave it to anyone else who isn't a trained professional.

5. **The marketplace is a consumer democracy**
   Consumers have options, so marketers have to tell them how to choose.

6. **Plan your destination**
   Make it where you want to be, not where you think you can get to. Once you have it, develop a strategy for getting there.

7. **Strategy is the boss**
   It controls the 'everything' in 'everything communicates'. You can decide to change your strategy, but you can't deviate from it.

8. **Marketing is a science**
   It is about experimentation, measurement, analysis, refinement and replication. You must be willing to change your mind.

9. **Figure out what is desirable**
   ...and make that what you deliver, or work out what

you can deliver and make that desirable. The former is a lot easier than the latter.

10. **Measure each brand and marketing region**

    Do it regularly and often, at least monthly. Marketing must create results.

11. **Ask questions**

    Be aware, insatiably curious and creative. Creativity is a process of destroying old ideas.

12. **Sameness doesn't sell**

    The value of your product will be determined by its differentiation from the competition in ways that are relevant to consumers.

13. **Use the right yardsticks**

    Focus on profit, not volume; on actual consumption, not share of market; and on share of future purchases, not brand awareness.

14. **Keep giving your customers more reasons to buy**

    You need them to come back more often and to buy more at higher prices.

15. **Market locally**

    You have to give all your customers something that appeals to them personally. Global brands are built out of many strong local brands.

16. **Fish where the fish are**

    Concentrate your sales efforts on consumers who are willing and able to buy your product. Segment the market to help you identify your most profitable targets.

17. Think SOB
Source of Business. Where will your next sale or profit come from?

18. Make sure everybody understands the strategy
...the destination and the business objectives. Then let them execute it.

19. Find the best available marketing professionals
...and create jobs around them. You've got to have the best people, not the best organisational chart.

20. Have a sense of urgency
...and work with passion. Otherwise, what's the use of getting up in the morning?

The one-sentence summary
When you start looking at exactly how much things cost and how much profit you are making you become a much better marketer.

The author has a bit of a chip on his shoulder about being disliked by advertising agencies, which can make some of his points defensive. The principles of new marketing aren't perhaps quite as revolutionary as the narrative makes them sound, but they do provide sound advice. Marketing is clearly not as dead as the title suggests, and it certainly hasn't reached the end of the road. It just needed some serious updating, and he wasn't the only one making the point.

Hang on a minute – it's back in new clothes

The New Marketing Manifesto JOHN GRANT

Around the same time that Mr Zyman was declaring the death of marketing, strenuous efforts were being made elsewhere to relaunch it in a new guise. In 1999 John Grant issued *The New Marketing Manifesto*. Subtitled *The 12 Rules for Building Successful Brands in the 21ˢᵗ Century*, the book took advantage of all the soul searching that surrounded the dawn of a new millennium to look at the underlying principles of successful modern brands.

He came up with 12 rules of New Marketing:

1. **Get up close and personal**
   Become intimate rather than public and formal, such as Nike's marketing strategy: getting closer to real people and real sport.

2. **Tap basic human needs**
   There are 15 fundamental human drives (sex, hunger, physicality, avoiding distress, curiosity, honour, order, vengeance, social contact, family, prestige, power, citizenship, independence and social acceptance). For example, Gucci repositioned from niche luxury to glamour.

3. **Author innovation**
   Brand identities should be fluid, not fixed, such as 35 years of brand leadership being turned around by the round tea bag.

4. Mythologise the new
Don't just reflect the status quo. Create possibilities
such as Clark's shoes introducing 'Act your shoe size'.

5. Create tangible differences in the experience
Sound, smell, touch, and taste, such as the beer market
working with Ice beer, with widgets and limes in the
top.

6. Cultivate authenticity
As opposed to false 'sincerity'. MTV Unplugged
effectively saved them from becoming what the author
calls McMusic.

7. Work through consensus
Forget targeting. Instead you should encircle and
involve audiences, such as the AIDS awareness
campaign designed to get shy couples talking about
condoms.

8. Open up to participation
Customers should be able to influence the brand, as
with Sainsbury's use of recipes.

9. Build communities of interest
Don't classify them, let them belong, in the same way
that Oddbins have applied the Wine Club concept to
store design and culture.

10. Use strategic creativity
Look at why? how? and where?, not standard media.
Gap used dance (a genre that transcends media) for
comfy, cool khakis.

11. **Stake a claim to fame**
    Do something memorable, because you can't buy
    fame. Richard Branson is a one-man marketing
    campaign for Virgin.

12. **Follow a vision and be true to your values**
    Set the goal and pursue it. When IKEA are presented
    with ideas their first question is always 'Is this us?'

These are all tenets that can be followed and applied to any
marketing issue. The contention is that New Marketing is
more creative than the old version. It treats brands as living
ideas that can transform people. It is entrepreneurial, more
humanist and less scientific. It favours constant change
over conservatism. It is part of a new consumer culture.

The one-sentence summary
**Brands are the new traditions, increasingly
playing the role that tradition used to play by
giving people ideas to live by.**

The book is an easy read, and well laid out with hundreds of
examples. There are lots of case studies if you need markets
to compare: IKEA, Tango, Pizza Express, French Connection, British Telecom, Egg and many more. Having been
written in 1999, unsurprisingly some of the ideas have
moved on somewhat, but that is not to detract from the
essence of what can be learned, and the manner in which
ideas are corralled into the 12 rules.

Working with the rules requires a certain method. Take
six simple questions and answer them in a sentence or less:

- *Why?* Why are we doing this marketing?

- *How?* Use the 12 rules to choose a method

- *Who?* Target audience

- *What?* Products and messages

- *Where?* Media selection

- *When?* Media schedule

This simple, inquisitive approach would certainly help to cut through much of the waffle and static in many a marketing plan. Combined with the ideas in the dozen interesting principles, they provide an excellent framework for the writing of a decent marketing strategy.

The old model: still working?

Meatball Sundae SETH GODIN

Seth Godin is one of the most popular writers on modern marketing matters, and in 2007 he published *Meatball Sundae*, subtitled *How New Marketing is Transforming the Business World (and how to thrive in it)*.

As is usual with this author, he chooses a deliberately enigmatic title that requires explanation. A meatball sundae is something messy, disgusting and ineffective, the result of two perfectly good things that don't go together. Meatballs are basic staples – the stuff that used to be marketed quite well with TV and other mass-market techniques. They are essentially commodities in the marketing sense – 'normal' products. The sundae topping is the new marketing, which looks appealing to traditional companies but is useless at selling meatballs.

For a century, successful organisations were built around traditional marketing tactics. New media alternatives have ended the guaranteed effectiveness of TV, and often deliver very fast results at almost no cost. But it doesn't work for everyone and asking what this stuff can do for you is most likely the wrong question. In other words, there is little point in a traditional company asking how new media can help support their existing structure and maintain business as usual. The right question is: 'If we're not growing how we would like, how can the business be altered?'

So, too many traditional companies that sell 'meatballs' are trying to jump on the new media bandwagon without considering how they can change their business. They will come unstuck because of their failure to acknowledge trends in new marketing, which are:

1. **Direct communication between producers and consumers**
   Organisations hear directly from customers far more often than they used to, thereby cutting out the middleman.

2. **Amplification of the voice of the consumer and independent authorities**
   Everyone can be a critic now, so service, quality and post-purchase issues are more critical than ever.

3. **Need for an authentic story as the number of sources increases**
   Saying one thing and doing something else won't work, because companies will be found out.

4. **Extremely short attention spans due to clutter**
   People arguably have too much choice and too many interruptions, so complex messages often do not get through.

5. **The Long Tail**
   As Chris Anderson has shown (see Chapter 1), in almost every market 'other' is the leading brand, so domination by hit products is fading as a force.

6. **Outsourcing**
   Almost everything can now be done cheaper elsewhere, to the point where talent and efficiency are triumphing over geography.

7. **Google and the dicing of everything**
   End-to-end solutions have been superseded by pick-and-choose, courtesy of search engines that break everything into small bits.

8. **Infinite channels of communication**
   The current media chaos is certain to get even worse.

9. **Direct communication and commerce between consumers and consumers**
   eBay was the start, and commerce between consumers is now commonplace, thereby bypassing many conventional companies.

10. **The shifts in scarcity and abundance**
    Scarce things are becoming more common, changing the degree to which companies can make a profit from what used to be hard to get.

11. **The triumph of big ideas**
In factory-based companies, small efficiency improvements can make a big difference, but the New Marketing context demands something bigger.

12. **The shift from 'how many' to 'who'**
For the first time marketers can concentrate on who is listening to their message, so they do not need to use a mass approach as a placeholder.

13. **The wealthy are like us**
Rich people now come from more diverse backgrounds, and may even include you.

14. **New gatekeepers, no gatekeepers**
Big organisations often got bigger, or maintained dominance, by doing business with the other big boys. They are no longer the exclusive gatekeepers to success.

The one-sentence summary
Don't fool yourself that your company has modernised just because you are doing something on the Internet – work harder at changing the business itself.

Interruption as a media thought no longer works. Consumers regard it as a form of SPAM and just hit delete or skip. The classic bell curve with volume in the mid price range has been replaced by an inverted one, where very cheap and expensive are the most fertile areas. So if your company is doing what it always did, but with a bit of new media activity bolted on, then success will be limited. We will look at this more in the next chapter with *Brand Manners*.

Oh-oh, it really is curtains

The End of Advertising as We Know it SERGIO ZYMAN

Our old friend Mr Zyman loves declaring that it's all over, and by 2002 he felt the need to do it again – this time directing his grim reaper message at advertising rather than marketing. As early as the introduction he claims that advertising doesn't work, it's a colossal waste of money and if you don't wise up, it could end up destroying your company (or your client's companies) and your brand. No immediate threat there then. And that's on the first page. Over two hundred pages later, he has had a go at most aspects of traditional advertising. Specifically, he asserts:

1. **Traditional advertising doesn't work, and is nothing to do with the standard notion of 30-second commercials.**

2. **Awareness doesn't sell, so there is no point in pursuing it in its own right. If you don't keep giving customers reasons to buy from you, they won't.**

3. **Advertising is a lot more than just television commercials. It includes packaging, spokespeople, employee relations and much more.**

4. **Loyalty is a perishable commodity – brands must change or die.**

5. **Fish where the fish are – stop looking for new users all the time.** (If this rings a bell, you're right. It's identical to point 16 in his previous book that we looked at earlier in the chapter.)

The one-sentence summary
Everything you do or don't do, or say or don't say, communicates something about your brand.

As we saw in his previous book, Zyman likes to nail some rules to the wall. In this one, he takes six old rules and writes new versions of them:

1. *Old:* **Give people budgets to spend wisely**
   New: **Give projects budgets, not people**

2. *Old:* **Awareness is king – assume people get it**
   New: **Awareness is irrelevant, so overcommunicate**

3. *Old:* **Promote from within, grow organically, and don't train**
   New: **Teach continuously and get regular transfusions**

4. *Old:* **Expand for success**
   New: **Maximise your existing assets**

5. *Old:* **Get lots of data**
   New: **Get relevant data**

6. *Old:* **Marketing is an expense**
   New: **Marketing is an investment**

Some of these points are more helpful than others. Decreeing a project budget rather than feeding the ego of a senior marketing operative makes sense, as does not pursuing awareness for the sake of it. The labour market idea of gaining regular transfusions has now become the norm, and maximising your existing assets appears fairly self-evident. Getting relevant data is a crucial point, because many companies these days have more data than they can possibly cope with, and frequently have no idea what to do with it all. Viewing marketing as an investment rather than an expense is an old chestnut that has been parroted for decades, and it is debatable whether boardroom decision makers pay much attention to the claim any more.

The book does however include some useful definitions of a brand:

- **a container for a customer's complete experience with the product;**

- **a bundle of functional and emotional benefits, attributes, experiences and symbols;**

- **the company's links to the likes, wants and needs of its customers;**

- **what keeps a company's loyal users coming back.**

Compare some of these ideas with those raised in Chapter 3. He also makes good sense on the business of crisis management:

- **have your response come from the top;**

- **tell the truth, tell it all, and tell it fast;**

- **do something to make it better;**

- **have a theme and stick to the script;**

- **know when to shut up;**

- **keep your PR people in the loop.**

This is all vital stuff, and can be compared with the advice of Roger Heywood in Chapter 3. As we now know, the author is the former Chief Marketing Officer of Coca-Cola. As such, he rather conveys the impression that he has seen and done it all, when in fact there are many circumstances in which his assertions would need to be handled quite carefully. For example, implementing his approach might upset the balance of teamwork because he is so opinionated on certain issues. The knack is to sift out the rhetoric to find the diamonds you need to provide inspiration.

It's all about the Interweb now, apparently

The Cluetrain Manifesto LEVINE, LOCKE, SEARLS, & WEINBERGER

And finally for this chapter, there are many who claim that marketing is now all about the Internet, and very little else. One of the first gangs to do so was Levine, Locke, Searls, and Weinberger in *The Cluetrain Manifesto,* first published in 2000, so we'll examine their thinking and see what effect it has had over the subsequent decade. When the World Wide Web and the Internet were first gaining widespread awareness, there was a NatWest advertisement featuring a slightly bemused man referring knowingly to the Interweb as the brave new dawn. And, in a way, it has become just that. However, a debate continues to rage about whether the Internet has totally replaced most other traditional media as the *only* really worthwhile marketing vehicle, or whether it is merely another channel, albeit a very success-ful and modern one.

The authors assert a number of important things:

1. The 'cluetrain' is simply following a chain of conversations on the Web.

2. It is the end of business as usual because these conversations have changed forever the way companies need to interact with their customers.

3. In fact, markets (customers) are now usually more intelligent than companies because they can exchange information faster.

4. Customers and employees are openly communicating so there are no secrets any more – one-way rhetoric from head office simply doesn't wash.

5. Companies that choose to ignore this are missing a massive opportunity.

The majority of this was pretty new in 2000, and in the main has proven to be right. Certainly, a lot of companies got a massive shock when they realised that the rise in online communication between consumers meant the end of their total control of communications. The Chief Executive who used to issue carefully sanitised statements at an Annual General Meeting and assume that the company image was sorted for the year had a hell of a surprise coming. His or her remarks would be completely deconstructed and posted on the Internet within minutes.

The one-sentence summary
It is the end of business as usual because online conversations have changed forever the way companies need to interact with their customers, so one-way rhetoric from head office simply doesn't wash.

It is interesting to consider that the appeal of the Internet is not so much the technology but people's desire to tell stories and communicate generally. It certainly must be true that an employee who tells the internal truth about a company can cause havoc, so companies need to know how to deal with it. The book includes an example of someone in Canada being overcharged for a car service, and the chain ends when an employee of the dealership he used explains how it is company policy to load prices. This sort of revelation puts the Internet on a par with the sort of investigative journalism previously only reserved for the best-resourced national papers.

There are 95 theses designed to ignite a debate. These can be read in five minutes and are a good source of stimulating quotes. Here are some highlights:

1. **Markets are conversations.**

2. **Markets consist of human beings, not demographic sectors.**

3. **The Internet is enabling conversations about human beings that were simply not possible in the era of mass media.**

4. **New networked conversations are enabling powerful new forms of social organisation and knowledge exchange to emerge.**

5. **As a result, markets are getting smarter, more informed, and more organised.**

6. **People have worked out that they get far better information and support from one another than from vendors.**

7. **There are no secrets. The networked market knows more than companies do about their own products.**

8. **Corporations do not speak in the same voice as networked conversations. To their online audiences, companies can sound hollow and flat.**

9. **Companies can now communicate with their markets directly. If they blow it, it could be their last chance.**

10. **Companies need to realise that their markets are often laughing. At them.**

As such, the book is a poignant reminder that communications should never be one-way. So there you have it: marketing still very much exists but has experienced something of a metamorphosis, adapting traditional channels and embracing the online world to come up with a new, shinier version of its old self. In the next chapter we will look at the murky world of brands and branding.

CHAPTER 2 WISDOM

- Marketing acts as a bridge between an organisation and the outside world, and is central to every company, but it doesn't have to be wrapped up in complicated jargon that confuses everyone.

- When you start looking at exactly how much things cost and how much profit you are making you become a much better marketer.

- Brands are the new traditions, increasingly playing the role that tradition used to play by giving people ideas to live by.

- Don't fool yourself that your company has modernised just because you are doing something on the Internet – work harder at changing the business itself.

- Everything you do or don't do, or say or don't say, communicates something about your brand.

- It is the end of business as usual because online conversations have changed forever the way companies need to interact with their customers, so one-way rhetoric from head office simply doesn't wash.

"Does it have to be a 'buzz' we create — or could it be just any kind of noise?"

CHAPTER 3. LOVEMARKS AND BUZZ: BRANDS AND BRANDING

What is branding? Categorising snowflakes

The Philosophy of Branding THOM BRAUN

If marketing is often accused of being a bit floaty, even worse can be levelled at the world of brands and branding. We will work through all the elements in a calm way as usual, but let's start with a charming and rather brilliant short book called *The Philosophy of Branding* by Thom Braun, first published in 2004. The content is extraordinary, as is the author, who combines being a serious writer on such heavy topics as Disraeli with directing Unilever's Global Marketing Academy. Oh, and he's an ordained priest.

The book is quite inspired and thoroughly original. It claims that there are strong links between philosophy and branding. It then works its way through the thinking of most of the major philosophers (in an accessible and light-hearted way), and expresses their views as though they were in charge of brands. This truly is, in its most literal sense, a review of the philosophy of branding. It eventually comes together in a list of top tips, which are:

1. **Assume that nothing is stable in the world in which your brand exists**
   It has to be managed on the basis of constant flux. (Heraclitus)

2. **Question everything**
   Take nothing for granted, and don't settle for anything that doesn't feel like the truth. (Socrates)

3. **Your brand should have two natures**
   Its superficial nature should always be changing, whilst keeping values that do not change over time. (Plato)

4. **Always ask what the brand is for**
   Unless there is a clear functional reason for purchase, consumers will fall out of love with it. (Aristotle)

5. **Identify the irreducible (certain) core of the brand**
   Understand deep-seated motivations and thought processes. (Descartes)

6. **A brand's tangible properties and how consumers think about it should not be managed as though they are separate**
   Distinguish between what is incontrovertibly true and what you would like to be true of the brand. (Spinoza and Leibniz)

7. **Hold fast to brand characteristics but make them in tune with the way the world is now**
   Don't get stuck in the past. (Locke)

8. **Don't be overly rational or logical**
   Reason has its limits – and it's not what drives consumer choice. (Hume)

9. **Reason is not the answer**
   Branding is about feelings and emotions. (Rousseau)

10. **Don't be fooled into thinking you can know everything about your consumers, markets and brands**
    You will only discover what your 'equipment' allows you to. Are you setting things up to tell you what you want to know? (Kant)

11. **Change is a process that can be understood and fast-forwarded**
    Pose a thesis, then the antithesis, and arrive at a synthesis. Resolve tensions through new and creative combinations. (Hegel)

12. **Values are at the heart of branding**
    Brand values should not just be attachments, but the driving force for what the brand can dare to become. (Nietzsche)

13. **Don't limit growth by only standing for one thing**
    Think of your brand as a tool that can have several uses. (Wittgenstein)

14. **Don't be swept along by processes ('the way we do it here')**
    Respect brands as individual and make bold decisions so they can express themselves. (Existentialism)

15. **Stop thinking in terms of certainties – they do not exist**
    See brand development as continuous problem solving and always look to replace current ways of thinking with better ones. (Popper)

The one-sentence summary
Brands and branding must be grounded in a rigorous and philosophical view of the way the world works.

This is certainly a highly original way of looking at brand management and should stimulate some new, more cerebral approaches. It is also an excellent way to acquaint yourself with the gist of most philosophical thinking, without reading the original impenetrable essays. The writing style is jargon-free, and short, so you can take it in quickly.

It is also fairly simple to apply the thinking, and back it up with intellectual stature. Perhaps not surprisingly though, a lot of the theories are contradictory, so you cannot use them all together as one approach. Every snowflake is different, and so are philosophical opinions. Finally, of course, none of the thinking here was ever applied to brands, so you have to check your relevance from time to time and keep a sense of perspective.

How should your brand behave?

Brand Manners PRINGLE & GORDON

In 2001 Hamish Pringle and William Gordon published *Brand Manners*, a wide-ranging review of important brands that suggested that companies need to align their internal and external brand values to build a self-confident organisation. They argued that customer perception of quality is a function of their pre-existing expectations of the brand, coupled with their experience when interacting with it. As a result, brand reputations can easily be ruined by one poor interaction – something much more closely linked to operations and on-the-ground reality than the rarefied area of marketing. This is a scary thought for marketers who like to proclaim what the brand is like, only to find that it isn't.

They outline the *Brand Manners* Improvement Cycle, which has five stages:

1. **Individual Behaviours**

   It's not enough to talk about missions and values. They have to be manifested in the concrete reality of individual actions.

2. **Encounters**

   Stay close to customers and staff, and engender an atmosphere of trust.

3. **Brand Promise**

   Technology and automation must not be allowed to remove humanity from brand interaction.

4. **Happy Surprises**

   Direct human interface generates defining gestures, pledges to customers, and moments of truth that should reflect the style of the brand.

5. **Feeling Good**

   The art of ensuring continually satisfied customers is to define your version of outstanding service, realise the importance of under-promising and over-delivering, and recruit in line with the brand's values.

The one-sentence summary

Customer perception of brand quality is a combination of pre-existing expectations and experience when interacting with it, so companies need to practise what they preach.

The cycle makes good sense and enables you to start a strategic debate that goes way beyond marketing communications. It makes sense – marketers can drone on all they like about what their brand stands for, but if the working reality is different, they are wasting their time. As such, the philosophy of the book is a useful antidote to macho marketing styles. Saying you are going to conquer the world is one thing – finding out that your brand or service is not up to scratch is a great humbler.

So the big question for all marketers is: are your customers completely satisfied as a result of their interaction with the employees who deliver your product or service? If the answer is no, or even maybe, then you need to make serious reparations before embarking on marketing that simply confirms, or even emphasises, the disconnect. Only when these points are attended to will your organisation have the self-confidence to the 'live the brand' properly.

This is crucial. How often has a company's handling of a customer's telephone response to an advertisement or direct mailing turned out to be a turn off? How often has a customer interaction with staff, or 'moment of truth', turned into a relationship killer rather than a loyalty builder?

Case histories in the book include Orange, Tesco, Coca-Cola, Ronseal, HSBC, and Pret A Manger, most of which can be directly applied to your own marketing circumstances. The format is in user-friendly chunks, with lots of diagrams that may help to inspire the content of other presentations. You could of course end up having a lot of theoretical debate about the behaviour in your organisation without making any particular progress on marketing issues, so the book provides a series of how-to guides at the back, for everyone from the CEO to the employee. The guide for Marketing Directors says:

- **have direct customer contact;**

- **create, sustain and evolve the dream;**

- live what customers experience, in real time;

- drive change into the organisation and make it stick;

- make marketing reflect the brand manners;

- make all employees reflect the brand manners;

- technology should be a customer-enriching servant to brand manners;

- front-line brand manners are crucial to customer service;

- the brand spirit should be used to ignite employee and customer enthusiasm.

All of this is a valid way of approaching how your brand is portrayed. You won't be able to control all of this, but you can have a bearing on it. Should you choose not to, it will take on a life of its own, and you may not like the result.

You'll have a brand image whether you like it or not

Manage Your Reputation, ROGER HAYWOOD

When it comes to enhancing and protecting your reputation, it usually pays to heed the advice of grown-ups who have been around and seen it all before. So it is with Roger Heywood, whose book first came out in 1994 entitled *Managing Your Reputation: How to Plan and Run Communications Programmes that Win Friends and Build Success.* As you can see, in those days they didn't go in for snappy titles.

The modern version is subtitled *How to Plan Public Relations to Build and Protect the Organisation's Most Powerful*

Asset, the implication being that reputation is indeed your most powerful asset. Most marketers would probably agree with that, and this is where we try to forge a link between brand image and Public Relations. The book outlines the basic principles of PR, how the direction must be set from the top, and how to design and measure every type of programme. It decrees three fundamental principles:

- **the attitude of someone taking a decision can be more important than the logical elements;**

- **a spontaneous reaction to your company or brand (the 'Pub Test') can be a decent measure of public relations;**

- **the best corporate behaviour is likely to be the most profitable.**

Asserting that your company or brand reputation is everyone's responsibility might enable you to start deeper strategic conversations with your colleagues, and help to make PR and marketing indivisible. Every practitioner's element to plan a good PR programme is here: developing the brief, writing the plan and measurement. There are whole chapters on public affairs, corporate and investor relations, issues and crisis planning, so this is a good place to start if you are confronted by issues in any of those areas.

There is also a section on how to develop an effective PR structure in an organisation, which summarises the thinking of all the industry bodies, and another on how clients should choose agencies, which should certainly be read as a reminder before any pitch or re-pitch.

The one-sentence summary
All organisations must behave impeccably and manage their public relations with intelligence if they are to safeguard their reputation.

Hundreds of appropriate ways of behaving flow from this central thought. For example:

1. **Choose your words carefully**
   An ill-chosen word can lose the argument, so think carefully before you speak, or issue a statement.

2. **Understand the other point of view**
   Experienced managers know the dangers of basing decisions only on personal observation.

3. **Encourage advice you do not want to hear**
   Overpowering management bullies advisers into submission, usually to their own detriment.

4. **You learn nothing when you are talking**
   Transmitting your message is one thing. Understanding and dealing with someone else's is altogether different.

5. **Consider the journalist's point of view**
   They are moved and motivated by the same things that apply to us all. Treat them properly and with consideration.

6. **Distinguish between aims and objectives**
   An aim is a direction in which progress is to be made, and an objective is a specific point to be reached.

As with many books that are closer to a textbook than an opinion-based piece, you are best off lifting out the chunks that suit your particular needs, rather than reading it end to end, although you may wish to do that too if you are new to PR altogether. There is no revolutionary thinking here – it is more like a manual of good practice.

Successful PR can be generated using a formulaic approach, but the best PR relies on some sort of spark or connection. This may be a natural feature of the brand, in which case the PR task will be significantly easier. If, however, your brand is much like any other, then you will need to work particularly hard at generating smart ideas in this area. These days this is often called 'buzz'.

Can you create a buzz around your brand and, if so, how?

Buzz SALZMAN, MATATHIA & O'REILLY

This is such a tricky area. Many good men and true have bitten the dust trying to achieve 'buzz' and notoriety for their brand, only to find that, despite intensive efforts, their profile is no better than any competitor. Here's the basic conundrum: buzz, word of mouth and favourable endorsement by advocates and ambassadors can be as elusive as hen's teeth. You want everybody to recommend your brand, but you can't force them. So you try to generate ideas that coerce them. That way, it looks as though they have reached a favourable opinion about your brand of their own accord.

In these days of highly structured PR, brand placement and endorsement campaigns, that is very rarely the case, but it doesn't stop marketers from trying. Everyone has a different definition of buzz, but according to Salzman,

Matathia and O'Reilly, who published a book of the same name in 2003, it has to be organic, centred on conversational value, peer driven and spread outwards from trend setters to trend spreaders and on to the mainstream. Others think the term has evolved. It used to mean anything the marketer does to make people talk about their brand. Now it may be more thoughtful and strategic than that, although there are still those who believe that it can never be achieved by an orchestrated effort.

According to the authors, the only thing consumers trust these days is personal experience. Word of mouth (WOM) should be renamed WORM because of the way it insinuates itself into the conscious (others have since renamed this Word of Relevant Mouth). They define a Buzz Continuum, which runs from the lunatic fringe (2 per cent), to the Alphas (8 per cent), to the Bees (20 per cent), to the mainstream (50 per cent), to the laggards (20 per cent). This sequence is simply a spectrum of early to late adoption of a product or service.

The book offers four springboards to generate buzz:

1. **Cultivate a culture of creativity**
   So-called 'silver bullet' ideas are generated by successful companies who reward creativity.

2. **Give 'em (consumers) what they always wanted (even if they don't know it)**
   Clever brands identify and launch products or services that appear to come out of nowhere and answer a need we might not have been conscious of.

3. **Capture the moment**
   Brands that capture accurately and viscerally the

feeling of the moment become the symbol or point of reference for that which they have encapsulated.

4. Challenge the conventions
Rules are made to be broken and conventions beg to be challenged. Good buzz does both.

The one-sentence summary
Generating word of mouth is the cheapest way to generate brand publicity, but you have to start it.

Much of buzz marketing apparently lies in the critical zone between 'best kept secret' and 'everyone's doing it', which may or may not help the hard-pressed marketer trying to deploy this approach. It is certainly worth trying to explain and categorise a phenomenon that plays a large part in modern marketing but it is quite hard to describe in absolute terms. The authors acknowledge the similarity of their suggestions to those in *The Tipping Point* (see Chapter 4) and try to build on it by explaining the role of superconnectors (people who are really good at linking others together), and by adding a degree of quantification and case history to the concept. As we will see, one of the great difficulties of all this is that it is all very well to say that you plan to create buzz or a tipping point, but quite how you achieve it is another matter altogether.

As such, the thinking is not so much earth-shatteringly original as a very comprehensive reorganisation of lots of other related work that covers influencers, tipping points, and how to seed trends in influential minorities in order to ignite mass acceptance. Commendably, it is also honest enough to include advice on how to handle negative buzz as well as generate the positive type – a form of crisis manage-ment that may be required if buzz efforts have gone spec-tacularly wrong.

Many questions remain in connection with this least tan-gible of all media, not least of which is precisely why people choose to be brand advocates, and whether it has any bearing at all on their long term loyalty.

Can you engender loyalty beyond reason?

Lovemarks KEVIN ROBERTS

This was the rather enigmatic question posed in 2004 by Kevin Roberts, worldwide CEO of arguably the most famous advertising agency in the world, Saatchi & Saatchi. What is a lovemark? You may well ask, and to answer that question we have to bury deep into the bowels of the agency's meth-odology. Here we go.

Picture two axes: one runs from low to high respect, the other from low to high love. Both words are of course being used in connection with brands. Here are the four types of brand that emerge when plotted on the graph:

1. Low respect, low love

This is the home of commodities. Bulk goods like steel, gravel and sand, as well as functional services such as brokerages and banks.

2. Low respect, high love

This is the 'fad zone' – the thing that everyone must have today, but has forgotten about tomorrow.

3. High respect, low love

This is where most major brands become stuck. They

may be great products and services but they are fixed on '-er' claims such as brighter, stronger, faster, and cheaper that have lost their currency. Nowadays, people want more than this.

4. High respect, high love
Emotional connections, seductive attitude and irresistible appeal all add up to Lovemarks. This is where you want your brand to be.

This all makes sense, until we arrive at the lovemarks word. What does it mean? The book claims that the idealism of love is the new realism of business. By building respect and inspiring love, business can move the world. Once there were products, then trademarks, then brands, and now lovemarks. For great brands to survive, they must create 'loyalty beyond reason', a trait that is indelibly associated with lovemarks. The secret is to use mystery, sensuality and intimacy to engender it. It's the consumers, not the companies, who really own the lovemarks.

If you have veered off at this point, bear in mind that the book is only attempting to redefine brand thinking, and is thought-provoking in its attempt to do so. Language is a strange animal, and the word lovemark has attracted some derision in its own right. Let's try to anchor this thinking in some solid points that the book raises:

1. Warning signs
You can tell when brands are descending into generic behaviour – that is, when they start being too consistent, interchangeable, impersonal, abundant, homogenous, and offering the lowest price. Is this your brand?

2. **Many brands are out of juice**
   This is an interesting notion. Is your brand worn out from overuse, no longer mysterious, can't understand the new consumer, struggling with good old-fashioned competition, captured by formula, or smothered by creeping conservatism?

3. **Human beings are powered by emotion, not by reason**
   The essential difference between emotion and reason is that emotion leads to action while reason leads to conclusions. Is your brand too reasonable?

4. **Primary emotions are critical**
   These are joy, sorrow, anger, fear, surprise and disgust, but they can be outstripped by more complex secondary emotions such as love, guilt, shame, pride, envy or jealousy. How many of these does your brand deploy?

5. **Some truths about love**
   Humans need it. It means more than liking a lot. It is about responding, about delicate intuitive sensing. It takes time and it cannot be commanded or demanded. Does your brand get close to this at all?

6. **A picture may be worth a thousand words**
   ...but terrific stories are right up there with them. A great story can never be told too often. Does your brand have a story to tell?

7. **Great ideas, like humour, come from the corners of the mind**
   That's why humour can break up log-jams in business and personal relationships. Go out on the edge. That's where you'll find the germ of an idea for your brand.

The one-sentence summary
Creating loyalty beyond reason requires emotional connections that generate the highest levels of love and respect for your brand.

When you strip it all down, this is decent thinking, but wrapped in more ethereal words than most of us are used to. Sometimes you have to look below the froth to see the meat in the soup, if you see what I mean. If you are going to pursue this more emotionally-based approach, then you are going to have to let go of any latent command and control attitudes because you will not be able to transmit to your customers in the old-fashioned way. Instead, you will be rooting around for more atavistic and visceral attributes that you can mobilise in your brand's favour. If that idea appeals, then read on.

Stop being a control freak: new ways to look after your brand

The Brand Innovation Manifesto JOHN GRANT
By 2006 John Grant, whom we encountered in the previous chapter, had thoroughly updated his view, so he published *The Brand Innovation Manifesto.* As far as he is concerned, the days of big image branding are over, and that includes the USP (unique selling point), brand essence, and cultural trends research, none of which do the job any more.

A quick word on these concepts so that we are all clear. The USP was first proposed as a theory in the early 1940s to explain how successful advertising campaigns made unique points to customers that convinced them to switch brands.

Today the term is used more loosely to refer to any aspect of a brand that differentiates it from others. Many marketers today believe that the USP concept is irrelevant because brands no longer have anything unique about them.

Brand essence is one of many phrases used to describe the core of what the brand is all about. You can imagine all the other types of words used in this way: core, soul, spirit, heart, vision, values, distillation – the list is near endless. Cultural trends research does what it says on the tin, and the author's point is that the idea that you can anticipate and ride the wave of a trend to ensure brand success is pretty much old hat.

Instead, he suggests, brands should be seen as clusters of cultural ideas, many of which can be contributed by consumers and other brands as well as the brand owners. The main concept in the book is the 'brand molecule', a modular structure to which new ideas can be added regularly. Instead of being a brand onion or pyramid shape, this is a series of interconnected brand ideas that look like many Olympic rings joined together. The number of circles will vary depending on how fertile the brand is. So for example the Beck's Bier brand molecule has the beer and German art expo in the centre. Radiating out to the edges are BritArt, the ICA prize, Slug and Lettuce contest, seeded in hip bars, drink sponsor openings, the bottle, iconic posters, artist special editions, and purity and heritage. The idea is that no single element dominates, and the brand can radiate and interlink with other ideas as appropriate. This type of map effectively becomes the new brand strategy.

He offers 32 types of brand idea that can be stolen or cross-pollinated to reinvigorate tired brands. These are all based on the idea of establishing a cultural logic as the basis of a brand strategy. Brand activities can be wide-ranging so long as they have a well-considered central theme based on this cultural logic. So the question you may wish to ask is: what is your brand's cultural logic? If yours is stuck in a strategic rut, you could do worse than try drawing up your own brand molecule, using any number of his 32 brand elements. These are:

- *New traditions* – habit, spectacular, leadership and organisation ideas
- *Belief systems* – cognitive, appreciation, faith, and Atlas ideas
- *Time* – regressive, now, nostalgia and calendar ideas
- *Herd instincts* – initiation, crowd, clan and craze ideas
- *Connecting* – co-authored, socialising, cooperative and localised ideas
- *Luxury* – concierge, plenty, exclusive and exotic ideas
- *Provocative* – erotic, cathartic, scandal and radical ideas
- *Control* – personalised, in-control, competition and grading ideas

The one-sentence summary
Build your brand, redefine the market and defy convention by generating a brand molecule instead of an old-fashioned unique selling point.

There isn't room here to elaborate on all 32 ideas. Suffice to say that it is helpful to bear in mind that few strategies are truly original – there is no sin in looking at other markets for inspiration and trying to apply the same thinking to yours. Be aware that the brand molecule idea could quickly run out of control if not carefully handled (although some element of ceding control may actually be beneficial). A random set of thoughts drawn as though they are connected, when in truth they are not, will not help your brand. So consider loosening the reins of your brand control, and try introducing co-authored ideas that will give it fresh stimulus.

CHAPTER 3 WISDOM

- **Brands and branding must be grounded in a rigorous and philosophical view of the way the world works.**

- **Customer perception of brand quality is a combination of pre-existing expectations and experience when interacting with it, so companies need to practice what they preach.**

- **All organisations must behave impeccably and manage their public relations with intelligence if they are to safeguard their reputation.**

- **Generating word of mouth is the cheapest way to generate brand publicity, but you have to start it.**

- **Creating loyalty beyond reason requires emotional connections that generate the highest levels of love and respect for your brand.**

- **Build your brand, redefine the market and defy convention by generating a brand molecule instead of an old-fashioned unique selling point.**

CHAPTER 4.
AFFLUENZA, HERDS AND QUIRKOLOGY: MYSTERIOUS CONSUMER BEHAVIOUR

People do some strange things

Quirkology RICHARD WISEMAN

Now we are going to take a look at the mysterious world of consumer behaviour. Why do people do what they do, and what bearing, if any, can marketing have on their actions? People do some very strange things, as explained by Richard Wiseman in his book *Quirkology,* which came out in 2007. In a strict sense, such a book has no direct relevance to the discipline of marketing. And yet it does, because psychology and the quirky science of everyday life have a deep bearing on consumer behaviour and as such lie at the heart of business understanding. If this could truly be unravelled and demystified, then marketers would either have it made, or not be required at all.

There is a reason for pretty much everything, so we are entitled to ask how our surnames influence our lives, why women should have men write their personal ads, and why people in Delhi are more helpful than Londoners. Some of the findings are hilarious, and include:

1. **Birth sign has no effect on behaviour at all, until people learn what their sign is and start behaving that way.**

2. **People can, within reason, choose when they die based on significant dates such as birthdays, and whether their inheritance will fall into a new tax year.**

3. **People can be made to remember things that they have never experienced.**

4. **The original idea of six degrees of separation has now gone down to four.**

This sort of stuff should be investigated more frequently by marketers, because it is real. Theoretical constructs about how consumers will respond to marketing initiatives are all very well, but it is much more revealing to see what they actually do when left to their own devices. The author has conducted thousands of experiments that either challenge our preconceptions or provide new answers to age-old questions. These include:

1. **People would rather wear a sweater that has been dropped in dog faeces and not washed, than one that has been dry-cleaned but used to belong to a mass murderer.**

2. **The difference between a genuine and fake smile is all in the eyes – in a genuine smile, the skin around the eyes crinkles.**

3. **The best way of detecting a lie is to listen, not look – liars say less, give fewer details and use the word 'I' less.**

Extraordinary stuff. Having a greater awareness of these possibilities could certainly help many aspects of your life – personal, social and business. From a marketing perspective, the book not only demonstrates that people behave in some very peculiar ways, but also that there must be many more ingenious ways of measuring consumer behaviour than those currently deployed by the market research industry.

The one-sentence summary
People do some very strange things, so don't take anything for granted.

Although the book answers a lot of questions, it probably raises a lot more. There's nothing wrong with that. We have already established that marketing is a constant process of reinvention. The fascinating range of findings in this book is clearly intended to make the reader more interesting, but it could equally make you a trivia bore if not handled carefully. You need to find a blend between being interested in minutiae on the one hand, and channelling that interest into workable marketing insights on the other. If that sounds daunting, don't panic.

People panic when they are told to

Panicology BRISCOE & ALDERSEY-WILLIAMS

Another bizarre thing about people is that they panic when they are told to, particularly about things they do not understand, according to Simon Briscoe and Hugh Aldersey-Williams in their highly-informative book, *Panicology*, which came out in 2008. It explains what is worth worrying about and what is not, based on the true statistics rather than media hype. The media is, as we established in Chapter 1, entirely responsible for 99 per cent of what people think they know, whether accurate or not. Even the quickest glimpse at what lies within reveals the extraordinary extent to which statistics are manipulated and misrepresented by vested interests and the media.

Example facts include:

1. People in different countries fear different things

For Danes it's nuclear power, for Italians radiation from their mobile phones, and so on.

2. An affordable house price to household income ratio is 1:3

In London, this is over 1:6.

3. We all live longer and have better standards of living than ever before

...and yet so much copy is generated on the perils of imminent death.

All the scare stories, including overpopulation, murder rates, fish shortages, and obesity levels, are analysed and explained accurately. Once you have reviewed all of this, you will come away wondering why you are concerned about anything at all. And yet we carry in our heads a bucket of worry that we seem compelled to fill with whatever is available, and the media provides an endless supply of material. Of course, many commercial interests add the spurious authority of a survey to support what they wish to say, as we saw in the first chapter.

The authors believe we have now spawned a new IPOD generation: Insecure, Pressured, Over-taxed, and Debt-ridden. But help is at hand. They have generated a sceptic's toolkit to help you work out whether something is valid or not. Here it is:

1. Vested interest

Who has made this statement and why might they have done it?

2. Weasel words

Watch for emotive ones such as plague, inevitable and overdue.

3. Surveys
Who conducted it? Are they credible? Do they have an obvious motive?

4. Figures
Try to compare them. If the data isn't there, ask what is being obscured.

5. Percentages and actual numbers
Scaremongers use percentages.

6. Anecdote and statistics
Fears are spread by word of mouth and harrowing individual stories. Authorities use statistics to provide a counter argument, but the two are almost impossible to compare accurately.

7. Graphs and charts
Don't automatically believe them just because they look technical. They are capable of distortion like everything else.

8. Timeframe
Many data series have a long-run trend, a shorter cyclical variation and (often erratic) individual data points. Be aware of this and don't be tricked.

9. Why now?
Would this story be newsworthy at another time?

10. Defeatism
Be wary when being told that there is nothing we can do about something.

11. Scare snobs
Distrust scares where an elite is trying to deny others advantages they already enjoy.

12. Scenarios
Many studies model a range of future scenarios. Make sure the one you are looking at is not just the worst-case.

13. Accentuate the positive
Don't discount the possibility that many things may get better.

14. The big picture
It's bad if 100 people die of bird flu, but in a country of 60 million, this is very small. How many died of everything else?

15. A sense of proportion
Try to keep one, even if animated spokespeople can't. Keep calm and carry on.

The one-sentence summary
There will always be someone who wishes to generate fear and panic, but they are usually biased, ill-informed or just plain wrong.

This is a well-written and informative book with sections that allow you to get to any subject you want, but there is no sequence as such, so dipping in might suit if you have a particular subject in mind. It provides a comprehensive sweep of what people do in light of so-called information. Now let's have a look at what and why they buy.

People buy more than they need

Affluenza OLIVER JAMES
Enough JOHN NAISH

In Western society at any rate, people almost always buy far more than they really need. This may be good for marketers but perhaps less so for the purchasers. Two books, *Affluenza* by Oliver James and *Enough* by John Naish, attempt to work out what is going on to see what we can learn.

Affluenza, published in 2007, is not a book about communications but it provides deep insights into the psychology of humans and as such is important for consumer understanding. Affluenza is defined as a contagious middle class virus causing depression, addiction and ennui. This is an epidemic sweeping the world, according to the author, and in order to counteract it and ensure our mental health, we should pursue our needs rather than our wants – the majority of which are unsustainable.

There is a questionnaire at the beginning to establish whether you have the virus, and a manifesto at the end suggesting how it can be stopped. There are hundreds of examples from all over the world and sources from academic studies to demonstrate that this is not simply a biased rant, although it is certainly a polemic.

He outlines many possible vaccines to the affluenza virus, which include:

1. **Have positive volition**
   Don't just think positive – make choices.

2. **Replace virus motives**
   ...with intrinsic ones – do things for the right reasons.

3. **Be beautiful**

   ...not attractive – don't conform to a marketing ideal of beauty.

4. **Consume what you need**

   ...not what advertisers want you to want.

5. **Meet your children's needs**

   ...not those of little adults.

6. **Educate your children**

   Don't brainwash them.

7. **Enjoy motherhood**

   ...not desperate housewifery/househusbandry.

8. **Be authentic**

   ...not sincere.

9. **Be vivacious**

   ...not hyperactive.

10. **Be playful**

    ...not game-playing.

The one-sentence summary

Most middle class people have too much of everything, but it hasn't made them any happier.

In addition you need to sort out your childhood and reject much of the status quo in order to be a satisfied, unstressed individual. The book contains a pretty blistering condemnation of the advertising industry and goes so far as to recommend a total ban on exceptionally attractive models.

Because the author is a psychologist, he is prone to recommending therapy, which may not suit everybody. Willpower could be just as effective.

In his book *Enough* (subtitled *Breaking Free From the World of More*), John Naish makes a similar point, but with a different twist. He observes that our basic survival strategy makes us chase more of everything: status, food, information, and possessions. Now, thanks to technology, we've suddenly got more of everything than we can ever use. As a result, we urgently need to develop a sense of 'enough', and an ability to enjoy what we have, rather than a fixation with 'more'.

On the data and information front, he believes we are suffering from *infobesity*. Too much information causes stress and confusion and makes us do irrational things. Examples include:

1. **Twenty-four-hour news media suffers from an 'Elvis still dead' syndrome that distorts our view of the world to the point that we have forgotten what true news is.**

2. **A personal data diet creates time for proper thought and interaction.**

3. **Purchasing items gives us a dopamine rush but it wears off almost immediately. Thousands of women in particular routinely return everything on a Monday that they bought on Saturday. Retailers call them shoe-limics.**

The concept of *presenteeism* is interesting. This is where people spend hours at their desks not achieving anything because they are too tired, stressed, under-stimulated, distracted or depressed to be productive. Workaholics Anonymous is a new movement based on AA principles. In an extreme paradox, earning more simply increases discontentment.

If you don't know what 'enough' is, you are not free, he claims. Meanwhile, Corporate Stockholm Syndrome makes people believe that their overwork habits are driven by irresistible external forces. They then frown on normal timekeepers and make their lives a misery. *'All the gear but no idea'* applies to fair-weather sports enthusiasts but could equally be applied to many who cannot stop stockpiling possessions. Sixty per cent of adults only use half of the functions on their devices, and WILFing is a pointless form of shopping: *What Was I Looking For?*

Overall, both authors agree that we have far too many options and a torture of choice. Marketing is frequently cited as a guilty party here, and marketers should be acutely aware of that. So has all this consumption made us any happier? No it hasn't, but amazingly we always think things will be better in the future. Present quality of life is deemed to be 6.9 out of 10 (and guessed at 8.2 in five years' time). But when the time comes, it's still 6.9.

People always copy each other

Herd MARK EARLS
The Wisdom of Crowds JAMES SUROWIECKI

Are we all individuals, or do we simply copy each other all the time? Mark Earls, author of *Herd*, believes the latter – an idea explored further in *The Wisdom of Crowds* by James Surowiecki, who argues that the collected view of groups is usually more accurate than that of one supposed expert.

The central principle of *Herd*, published in 2007, is to challenge our assumption that the individual is the starting point from which to understand human behaviour. By focusing on group behaviour, or the 'herd', Earls believes that we have the key to a better understanding of human behaviour and better business and social policy initiatives to change it.

It is subtitled *How to Change Mass Behaviour by Harnessing Our True Nature*, and the main point is that, whilst most marketers are banging on about individual choice and one-to-one marketing, in fact everybody just copies, or is influenced by, other people. As such, most attempts by marketers to alter mass behaviour fail because they are based on a false premise. This is why most government initiatives struggle to create real change, why so much marketing money fails to drive sales, why mergers and acquisition programmes actually *reduce* shareholder value, and why most internal change projects don't deliver any lasting transformation.

The seven principles of Herd marketing are:

- *Interaction* (between people)

- *Influence* (of certain people)

- *Us-Talk* (the power of word of mouth)

- *Just Believe* (stand for something and stick to it)

- *(Re-)Light the fire* (overcome cynicism by restating the original idea)

- *Co-creativity* (let others join in)

- *Letting go* (you never were in charge of your brand)

If you are reading this book sequentially, you can now really see how all the themes start to come together. Earls believes that most of us in the West have misunderstood the mechanics (the 'how') of mass behaviour because we have misplaced notions of what it means to be human. We are, at heart, a 'we' species, but one suffering from the 'illusion of I'. This challenges most standard conceptions about marketing and urges the reader to rethink the whole thing, based on the conclusion that the most important metric for any business is the degree to which its customers influence each other positively. This idea has massive repercussions for anyone involved in marketing.

The one-sentence summary
Forget individual choice – people just copy each other, but crowds usually get it right.

So now we round out the picture with the views of James Surowiecki, who published *The Wisdom of Crowds* in 2004. Subtitled *Why the Many are Smarter than the Few,* his theory was first aired as a column in *The New Yorker* magazine. History tells us that when you want something done you turn to a leader: right? Wrong, he declares. If you want to make a correct decision or solve a problem, large groups of people are smarter than a few experts. When Charles Mackay wrote in 1841 about *Extraordinary Popular Decisions and the Madness of Crowds,* he presented an endlessly entertaining chronicle of mass manias and collective follies. This book proposes the opposite, and has huge implications for the way we run our businesses, structure our political systems, and organise our society.

If taken at face value, the book could change the way you think about human behaviour. His points include:

1. **In 1906 800 people guessed the weight of an ox. The average of their guesses was exactly right.**

2. **In 1968 a submarine was lost, and only when several scenarios were pieced together from many different sources did they find it.**

3. **On *Who wants to be a millionaire?* the experts (phone a friend) are right 61 per cent of the time, and the crowd 91 per cent.**

Scores of anecdotes and evidence of this type keep coming all the way through, so what can we distil for marketing purposes?

1. **The difference that difference makes**
   Tiny changes can make for mass acceptance.

2. **Monkey see, monkey do**
   Independence is important to intelligent decision-making.

3. **Putting the pieces together**
   Decentralisation (letting go of control) makes for better collective decisions.

4. **Shall we dance?**
   Coordination is possible in a complex world, as evidenced by how huge numbers of people successfully navigate their way round busy city streets.

5. **Committees, juries and teams**
   These do not make good decisions if they are led in a certain direction by the chairperson.

6. **Meet the new boss, same as the old boss?**
   Companies that coordinate their behaviour with that of
   their customers do better, such as Zara delivering new
   lines twice a week instead of once a fashion season.

This book is hard to classify because there are no clear sections so you have to burrow deep for these nuggets, but the
combined effect of herd behaviour and the wisdom of
crowds has significant bearing on how marketers should
approach markets and understand the collective decision-
making that shapes them.

People are usually right

Blink MALCOLM GLADWELL

We finish the chapter by looking at two concepts from the
highly popular Malcolm Gladwell. In *Blink,* he asserts that
people are usually right if they trust their instincts –
something marketers could learn from as they labour over
mountains of data and research. Gone are the days when an
experienced Marketing Director would use intuition and
experience to make an informed decision. Many are now
paralysed by too much data, and seem to prefer to be precisely wrong rather than roughly right.

In 2005, Gladwell claimed that our ability to 'know' something in a split-second judgement, without really knowing
why we know, is one of the most powerful abilities we
possess. A snap judgement made very quickly can actually
be far more effective than one we make deliberately and
cautiously. By blocking out what is irrelevant and focusing
on narrow slices of experience, we can read seemingly
complex situations in the blink of an eye. This is essentially

'thinking without thinking' – a powerful instinct that we would do well to deploy more frequently, if only we could trust it more.

He also introduced the theory of 'thin slicing' – using the first two seconds of any encounter to determine intuitively your response or the likely outcome to a situation – and demonstrated that this little bit of knowledge can go a long way, and is accurate in over 80 per cent of instances.

The book features scores of vivid examples in which peoples' first instincts have been right, but they cannot explain why. These include an art dealer identifying a fake statue that the Getty museum believes to be genuine, a tennis coach being able to predict every time when players are about to serve a double fault, and a psychologist accurately guessing years in advance if married couples will stay together or not.

This type of fresh thinking is a welcome counterpoint to a world in which too much reliance on proof and data has replaced hunch and instinct. The value of spontaneity is highlighted by the example of a forces commander who comprehensively beats better-equipped opposition in a US military exercise because he consistently does the opposite of what the computers predict. Marketers would do well to note this 'zig when they zag' approach, and use it as stimulus to initiate ideas that break away from the norm. He goes on to show that, strangely, it is possible to give 'structure' to spontaneity, by consciously going against the grain in order to generate an outcome that is surprising to the other party, but not to you.

The one-sentence summary
**Trust your first instinct, because a snap
judgement made very quickly can actually be
far more effective than one you make
deliberately and cautiously.**

This is thought-provoking stuff. There is a hitch though. Although the subject matter is fascinating, there are so many experts interviewed that the average marketer would not be able to enact any of the skills necessary to take advantage of the findings, other than the basic point that you should trust your first instincts more. As such, embracing the spirit of the idea carries more weight than any strict adherence to a methodology, because there isn't one.

Small things can make a big difference

The Tipping Point MALCOLM GLADWELL
In his first book from 2000, *The Tipping Point,* Gladwell shows that small things can make a big difference, thereby somewhat puncturing the bubble of those marketers who are always looking for the next big thing, the big idea, or pushing for a larger budget. None of these may be necessary for success, he claims. He explains and defines the 'tipping point' – the moment at which ideas, trends and social behaviour cross a threshold, tip and spread like wildfire. Just as one sick person can start an epidemic, very minor adjustments to products or ideas can make them far more likely to be a success. The overall message of the book is that, contrary to the belief that big results require big efforts that are beyond the capacity of the single individual,

one imaginative person applying a well-placed lever can move the world.

It is optimistic in outlook and suggests that individuals can make a significant contribution. It cites the example of Paul Revere who, in 1775, overheard a conversation and rode all night to warn Americans in Boston that the British would attack in the morning. The Americans were ready and defeated them.

He outlines three areas that are a good working template for all communications:

1. The Law of the Few
The idea that the nature of the messenger is critical.

2. The Stickiness Factor
The quality of the message has to be good enough to be worth acting on.

3. The Power of Context
People are exquisitely sensitive to changes of time, place and circumstance.

Experienced readers, and particularly those who have worked in media and advertising agencies, will immediately spot that these three areas aren't that original – they are roughly similar to the medium, message and target audience sections that can be found in any self-respecting campaign brief. That is not to do them down, because the language used may spur the writer of any brief on to more original thinking.

The one-sentence summary
One imaginative person applying a well-placed lever can move the world.

Finally though, a word of caution. It is easy to get distracted by the three groups of people whom he claims may start a tipping point:

1. *Connectors* (people who know a lot of people)

2. *Mavens* (those who accumulate knowledge, but are not persuaders)

3. *Salesmen* (people who are very persuasive)

These typologies have certainly captured the imagination of the marketing world, but they aren't really the book's central point. Those who work in PR and are keen to 'influence the influencer' find them particularly appealing, but identifying these types of people may get you no closer to actually starting a tipping point. All of which leaves the chapter finishing on a nicely-balanced conundrum: even if a marketing strategy overtly sets out to create a tipping point, it is probable that they are so idiosyncratic and hard to predict that such a marketing strategy may actually be impossible to enact. Food for thought, perhaps, as we venture into the world of creativity.

CHAPTER 4 WISDOM

- People do some very strange things, so don't take anything for granted.

- There will always be someone who wishes to generate fear and panic, but they are usually biased, ill-informed or just plain wrong.

- Most middle class people have too much of everything, but it hasn't made them any happier.

- Forget individual choice – people just copy each other, but crowds usually get it right.

- Trust your first instinct, because a snap judgement can actually be far more effective than one you make deliberately and cautiously.

- One imaginative person applying a well-placed lever can move the world.

"And this is our creative department."

CHAPTER 5.
CREATIVITY: CAN
YOU LEARN IT?

We are all born to play and create

The Play Ethic PAT KANE

We are now going to grapple with the tricky area of creativity. What is it? How do you know when an idea is 'creative'? Is creativity the sole preserve of the creative department or can anyone have a good creative idea? Can you learn it even if you do not believe that you are naturally creative? How long is a piece of string? So many questions. We will start by looking at the broad area of what creativity might be, and work our way through to find that there are some exercises and techniques that might help to generate worthwhile creative ideas.

We are all born to play and create, according to Pat Kane in *The Play Ethic,* and he should know because he also sings in the band *Hue And Cry.* They were massive stars in the late eighties and have recently made a comeback. As a suitable tribute I am playing one of their albums as I write. Published in 2004, the book suggests that politicians arguing consistently for a work ethic are missing the point. We are essentially designed to play.

We all think we know what play is (what we do as children, outside work, and for no other reason than pleasure), but understanding the real meaning of it would revolutionise and liberate our daily lives. Huge numbers of companies now make their money out of play elements – who is to say that is wrong? Play offers learning, progress, imagination, a sense of self, identity and contest. It is also the fermenting ground for exploring alternatives – the very essence of creativity. His ideas include:

1. **Your mind is a 'possibility factory' – use it**
   We will look at specific techniques to help do this later in the chapter.

2. **There is a new generation of Soulitarians and Lifestyle Militants**
   They are more interested in the quality of life, and what they do for a living, than the money.

3. **Poiesis is the act of producing something specified**
   Too few people can do this so we should cherish those who can.

4. **When work becomes too humane (nice to do), we do too much of it**
   This is a really interesting and slightly perverse notion, but appears to be true.

5. **Sick-related stress costs companies £370m a year in the UK**
   They should be more enlightened about job sharing and working from home to reduce this figure.

6. **Much so-called play (such as computer games) constitutes 'hard fun'**
   If they do not represent a challenge, they aren't considered to be good.

7. **'I think, therefore I produce'**
   This is an interesting new credo for people in the information age.

8. **Technology was supposed to make our lives easier**
   Instead it annihilates our time by intruding on every moment of the day – we need to offset this.

All of these observations inform the debate. Kane's contention is that we should have a play ethic, not the work ethic so beloved of hectoring politicians who seem determined to consign our lives to the proverbial grindstone.

The one-sentence summary
Play is the fermenting ground for exploring alternatives and as such is the very essence of creativity.

This book is a complicated and detailed read – perhaps the very opposite of what you might expect from a former pop star. In fact, it is superbly sourced and very thought-provoking, so prepare to be challenged. You could dip in, but it is more of a long essay or dissertation, so it is best to read it end to end.

Because it is very widely researched, you would have to work extra hard to track down all the lines of enquiry that it suggests – web links, support papers and so on. For an enthusiast, that might be a pleasure, and would undoubtedly lead to a fascinating trail of enquiry. For the majority in this time-pressed world though, I suspect you will make do with this summary. So now let's see if we can find a purpose for creativity.

Creativity is pointless without a purpose

Welcome to the Creative Age MARK EARLS
Having a good old play is absolutely fine, but creativity is pointless without a purpose, argues Mark Earls in *Welcome to the Creative Age* (2002). This seems a more than fair counterpoint, since one of the greatest criticisms of the

communications industry is random creativity for the sake of it, with little commercial result. The author is among many to spot that old-fashioned marketing is dead. It used to be about selling more than the other guy, but now it is mistakenly embraced as an organisational philosophy. In other words, most companies now have a marketing department, and as such 'do marketing', but that doesn't necessarily mean that they know what they are doing, or indeed whether they are doing it properly. They set up the systems and go through processes, but if creativity doesn't thrive on either of those, then they might not get anywhere.

Creativity is our greatest gift, but we don't always use it effectively, says Earls. Four big things have changed the face of marketing:

1. **There is too much of everything**
   Every market is over-supplied.

2. **The end of the consumer**
   People are now very confident and understand what marketing people are doing.

3. **The rise of the consumer as activist**
   If people don't like the way a company is behaving, they do something about it.

4. **The demanding employee**
   The company man is dead.

It is important for marketers to bear this in mind when considering creative concepts. The ideas themselves require careful scrutiny. Earls starts with *Creative Age Ideas*, and presents them with three main components:

- **they should assume that audiences are neither listening nor interested;**

- **they should not try to fit in (in fact they should usually challenge);**

- **they are often the result of strongly held beliefs, not rational analysis.**

These are then re-named *Purpose Ideas*: what counts is what you want to change about the world. In other words, what is your purpose?

The one-sentence summary
There is no point in pursuing creativity without a purpose.

The book tells you how to have ideas like this by identifying your purpose (not your positioning) and deciding on interventions (it's what you *do* that counts). These are important distinctions, because the marketing world is full of positioning statements, but they don't necessarily get the brand anywhere. Equally, marketing is plagued by too many meetings and too much waffle, so you can talk as much as you like but it is not until you actually do something that the creative idea can be shown as effective or dud.

There are lots of good mantras that could inspire, such as:

1. **Leave your agenda at the door**
   Those pursuing only one line of thought can often stifle creativity.

2. **The brand ties you to the past**
   Similar to breaking with your immediate past that we saw in Chapter 1.

3. **Benchmarking your way into a corner**
   Copying what the competition is doing rarely works.

4. **Control is an illusion we are better off without**
   You have never been in control of your brand, so don't pretend that you are.

This last point usually upsets marketing people, but it is becoming more and more true as networked communities on the Internet make their own collective decisions about what brands stand for, regardless of what gets written in the marketing department. The 'added-value banana' anecdote, in which one is packaged as a 'fresh banana snack' ideal to be eaten on the move (all of which we know already), is salutary about the insanity of much modern marketing. That's why there is a banana on the cover.

The book also contains views on why large numbers of advertising people don't actually know how advertising works, which might be unsettling if you work in the industry. *'Fact: most of the people in an ad agency are not paid to be inventive or creative but to manage and service the ad-factory machinery.'* Ouch. Any book that declares the death of something has to propose new ways forward. This one pretty much does, in as much as it explains how to put Purpose Ideas at the heart of your business, and aims to set you thinking for yourself. But that may just be the start of the difficult bit.

You can try emulating creative companies

Juicing the Orange FALLON & SENN
Marketing Judo BARNES & RICHARDSON

One way to embrace creativity is to try to emulate creative companies, so now we look at that possibility by studying two very different books. *Juicing the Orange,* by Fallon and Senn, was published in 2006, and subtitled *How to turn creativity into a powerful business advantage.* They look at a lot of organisations and conclude that they have more creativity than they realise, but that they inadvertently stifle it, or channel it in the wrong directions. By contrast, in *Marketing Judo,* Barnes and Richardson explain how to build a business using brains rather than budget. We will combine the best advice that these authors have to offer.

Fallon and Senn's central point is that marketers should identify one critical business problem that needs solving, and then rigorously unearth insights that lead to a spectacular solution. They propose Seven Principles of Creative Leverage:

1. **Always start from scratch.**

2. **Demand a ruthlessly simple definition of the business problem.**

3. **Discover a proprietary emotion for your brand.**

4. **Focus on the size of the idea, not the size of the budget.**

5. **Seek out strategic risks, not the safety of common ground.**

6. **Collaborate or perish.**

7. **Listen hard to your customers (then listen some more).**

Starting from scratch is probably harder said than done, but more marketers should certainly attempt to do it, or at least investigate doing it, lest they be constantly struggling with legacy issues that hinder their work. The principles at the heart of the book should resonate with anyone involved in any form of creative marketing:

- **Creativity is an increasingly essential business tool**

- **You can't buy creativity, but you can unlock it**

- **Creativity is not an easy path to walk but the rewards are worth it**

The one-sentence summary
When considering creative ideas, concentrate on the size of the idea, not the size of the budget.

In *Marketing Judo* (2003), Barnes and Richardson pick up the theme. You don't need a big budget to build a brand, they claim. The authors rejuvenated the Harry Ramsden's brand and now run their own company, also called Marketing Judo. The principles of judo, where brains matter more than brawn, can help tremendously in this context (*Ju* means flexible and *Do* means way).

They propose seven stages (how many times do we see seven stages?):

1. **Get the basics right**
   Don't spend on marketing till the basics are working.

2. **Pick the right partner**
   Carefully choose staff, advisers, celebrities, and other brands with whom to work.

3. **Choose the right opponent**
   Choose sloths, not Geesinks (see below).

4. **Get the crowd on your side**
   Create your own fan club by generating emotional leverage.

5. **Use your size to your advantage**
   Keep the company fit, move fast, stay focused, and generate ideas that suit this mentality.

6. **Do the unexpected**
   Unpredictability can be harnessed to create competitive advantage.

7. **Keep your balance**
   There are huge benefits in planning for the unexpected.

The point about choosing your competition is well made. Spotting corporate sloths is a good way to identify competition that you can actually beat. By contrast, don't choose Geesinks. Anton Geesink was a 6' 6" judo player who beat everyone in the 1964 Olympics and forced the introduction of weight classification for the first time. How many marketers thump the table and declare that they are going to smash the brand leader, only to discover that they would have been far better picking off a weaker adversary?

There are plenty of examples of those who get it right: Pret A Manger, Kettle Foods, Cobra Beer, and Eddie Stobart. Walkers is cited as a Geesink that you wouldn't want to go up against. The book is short and pithy, and the method can be followed and applied simply. For example, try having a Brains Day instead of a Budget Day if you want to generate creativity that will get you somewhere.

Drawing the thinking in both books together, the message is to use your size to your advantage and squeeze more juice out of your metaphorical orange. The orientation is all about what to do when you have little or no budget, which should not be viewed as an insurmountable impediment. There is much to be learned from how creative companies conduct themselves.

You can try applying some universal rules

The 22 Irrefutable Laws of Advertising, MICHAEL NEWMAN

Rules, rules, rules. Should you adhere to them or ignore them? One book attempts to let you do both. *The 22 Irrefutable Laws of Advertising* by Michael Newman, published in 2004, is subtitled *...and When to Violate Them.* So there's your get-out clause. You can try applying some universal rules, but if you don't like them you can break them.

The book is a series of essays by the great and the good including Dave Trott, Kevin Roberts, James Lowther, and M.T. Rainey, each one generating its own law. Most of these are self-explanatory: the laws of simplicity, positioning, consistency, selling, emotion, love, experience, relevance, humour, disruption, jump, fascination, irreverence, taste, topicality, chat, nice, negativity, execution, and evolution.

Others are more oblique and require explanation:

The Law of the Silver Elephant
This is the intent to produce something that has never been done before, and the act of carrying it out.

The Outlaw
Everything we have told you is a lie, including this. In other words, feel free to ignore everything the book advises, should you wish to break all the rules.

There are lots of different opinions here, so you are not going to be reading 200 pages all making the same point. Coherent narrative is out; point and counterpoint are in. Instead you will be looking for angles – some inspiration or a jumping off point. The author sets up a decent introduction grappling with the tricky business of how to catch lightning in a bottle (the elusive search for genuine creativity), and 'how bad is it, doc?' (a quick rundown on the problems facing the advertising industry, which would make a book in its own right).

Each of the laws effectively has a natural nemesis, so at the end there is a list of irresponsible crimes against advertising, that always violate profits. The crimes are:

1. Research
Once described as looking in the rear-view mirror of a fast-moving car.

2. Logic
Look for the emotionally real answer, not the logically right one.

3. Familiarity
Familiarity breeds inertia.

4. **Self-importance**
   Don't patronise your customers. The consumer is not a moron – she is your wife.

5. **Against humanity**
   Don't go for ideas that inhabit their own world of gloss and cheesiness.

6. **Atheism**
   Good creative ideas cannot lack an opinion.

7. **Strangulation by data**
   Advertisers are overwhelmed with data and yet starved of understanding, connection, magnetism and humanity.

8. **Interference**
   This is the insanity of barking when you have a dog. Let the experts get on with it and don't meddle.

9. **Pitching for free**
   Fear is a lousy climate in which to generate good creative ideas.

10. **Commoditisation of the creative product**
   Ideas have become devalued because of price-cutting and wheeler-dealing in the industry.

The one-sentence summary
It is possible to codify the rules that make a great idea, but equally you might want to ignore them all in search of originality.

Any marketer experiencing a blockage in their communications thinking should be able to dip into one of these theories and pull out a new approach to their issue. Particularly useful is Dave Trott's binary brief, which is constructed simply by choosing one of only two alternatives to each of the normal questions you would expect to address in a creative brief (not multiple options). These are:

1. **What does the advertising need to achieve?**
    a. Grow the market
    b. Go up against whoever is bigger than us

2. **Who should we target?**
    a. Current users to buy more
    b. People who have never tried it to switch to us

3. **How do we do it?**
    a. Do we have a genuine Unique Selling Proposition?
    b. Should we be selling the brand?

That couldn't be simpler, and is an excellent way to get a marketing strategy out of a muddle if it has all become too convoluted, which happens more often than you might expect. Laws may polarise opinion, but if they are viewed as being there to be challenged or broken, then they can represent a very useful springboard. Books of this type are always a bit schizophrenic about whether all the laws should be obeyed, or ignored – the choice is yours.

You can try some stimulating methods

The Art of Creative Thinking JOHN ADAIR
Flicking your Creative Switch PEASE & LOTHERINGTON
So now is the time to get to the heart of what this chapter is all about: can you learn creativity? Well, you might well be

able to, and the best way to find out is to try some of the techniques that have helped many others to be creative. *The Art of Creative Thinking* by John Adair, something of a legend in this area, was first published in 1990. He believes that once you understand the creative process you can train yourself to listen, look and read with a creative attitude. His techniques include:

1. **Use the stepping stones of analogy**
   Use normal things to suggest new uses.

2. **Make the strange familiar and the familiar strange**
   Analyse what you don't know about something that you know well.

3. **Widen your span of relevance**
   Many inventions were conceived by those working in other fields.

4. **Be constantly curious**

5. **Practice serendipity**
   The more you think, the more it appears you are in 'the right place at the right time'.

6. **Make better use of your Depth Mind**
   Trust your sub-conscious to sort things out and generate solutions once you have 'briefed it'.

7. **Learn to tolerate ambiguity**

8. **Suspend judgement**

9. **No one should wait for inspiration**
   You have to make it happen.

This rather brilliant short book was originally written 20 years ago, so it is not riddled with modern jargon or method. It just tells it straight: chance favours the prepared mind. By keeping your eyes open, listening for ideas and keeping a notebook, you can capture stimuli as they occur. It is full of inspirational comments from artists, scientists and philosophers:

'I invent nothing; I rediscover.'
RODIN

'Everything has been thought of before, but the problem is to think of it again.'
GOETHE

'Discovery consists of seeing what everyone has seen and thinking what nobody has thought.'
ANON

The one-sentence summary
You can be more creative if you train yourself to think differently.

Pease and Lotherington, in *Flicking your Creative Switch* (2003), say that everyone can be creative, regardless of whether they think they are. They describe creativity variously as 'the spark that ignites new ideas', 'the infinite capacity that resides within you', and 'shaping the game you play, not playing the game you find'. Good ideas arise when we take something we already know (light bulb number one) and consider it in relation to another thing we already know but which is unrelated (light bulb number two). Merging them creates light bulb number three – the new idea.

ROI is used to stand for Relevance, Originality and Impact. Your ideas won't work if they do not have all three. Barriers to creativity have been placed in our way since childhood: *don't be foolish, grow up, work before play, do as you're told, don't ask questions, obey the rules, be practical* and so on. We need to ignore all these and get on with it. He offers six techniques that you can use to generate creative ideas:

1. Random Word

Take a noun randomly from somewhere and apply it to the subject. You can also use pictures.

2. Eyes of Experts

Choose three respected experts from other fields and consider how they would deal with your issue. There is a variation of this technique called Industrial Roundabout where you view it through a different category.

3. What's Hot?

Use popular current things to appeal to your audience.

4. Curly Questions

Use analogies, speculation, role reversal and imagination to re-phrase the issue at hand so that more original answers emerge.

5. Exaggeration and Depravation

Over-exaggerate the benefits of a product, or push to ludicrous extremes what happens if it isn't present.

6. **Exquisite Corpse**
   Based on surrealist thinking, different people randomly
   select five words to create a sentence in the pattern
   adjective/noun/verb/adjective/noun. Eg. *The peculiar
   bicycle swims a brilliant banana.* Each word is then
   scrutinised to review the problem.

The book even explains the origin of the dreaded phrase
'thinking outside the box'. The Gottschaldt figurine, or nine-
dot game, requires you to join all the dots without taking
your pen off the paper. You can't solve it if you view it as a
box, so you must think outside it. So now you know. Between
them, these two books provide a significant arsenal of
methods to stimulate creativity. You might be able to do this
on your own, but you might want to involve other people.

You can try involving lots of people

We-Think CHARLES LEADBEATER

Finally, modern thinking suggests that you can try to create
something by involving lots of people, in what is often
called co-creation. The classic example of this is *We-Think*,
by Charles Leadbeater, who effectively wrote a best-selling
book by getting 257 other people to help him write it on the
Internet. That's the modern way, and nobody seems to
worry that it may not entirely be the author's original work,
although he takes the bulk of the credit and gets the speak-
ing engagements as a result.

Part of the reason for this is the generous spirit of sharing
that pervades information and advice on the Internet. The
majority of people are happy to offer up their ideas for free.
According to Leadbetter, the future is us, via mass

collaboration, not mass production. The rallying call of the Web is for shared power that makes society more open and egalitarian. There has been an unparalleled wave of democratic, productive and creative participation online, and this book is itself an example.

The generation growing up with the Web will not be content to remain spectators. They want to be players and their slogan is *'we think therefore we are.'* Self-determination is a powerful thing. In 1998, BT had failed to get its field engineers to work harder and so set up a *Freedom to Choose* scheme whereby the engineers scheduled their own work. After three years they were working two hours a week less and earning significantly more. Productivity was up five per cent and quality eight per cent. The moral is that if you let people sort things out themselves they do a responsible, and often better, job. This particular example is certainly beguiling, but the claim can't be universally true.

Nevertheless, there is definitely appeal in the new mantra of *you are what you share*, and the author works through numerous examples of how this works in the modern world, all facilitated by the Web. The roots of we-think reside in a strange mixture of online contributors:

1. **The academic**
    ...who brings a belief that knowledge develops through sharing ideas and testing them through peer review.

2. **The hippie**
    ...who brings a deep scepticism about all sources of authority.

3. The peasant

...who favours shared use of communal facilities and resources.

4. The geek

...who offers to realise their dreams by networking them together.

When you put all this together, you have a powerful blend that can create original ideas and solve most problems. The way it works is to start with the core, then get other people to contribute to it. They then connect over it, collaborate, and create something. These are the Five Cs, and this is what they could mean for learning and harnessing creativity:

1. Core

Everything has to start somewhere, so sketch out your best effort at creating the idea.

2. Contribute

A successful creative community has to attract the right mix of people, and the bigger it is the more helpful the response you are going to get.

3. Connect

People are innately keen on joining in. You need to foster this phenomenon and channel the flow of information and ideas.

4. Collaborate

A mass of contributions does not amount to anything unless together they create something constructive and creative. If you are the instigator, you will need to manage this.

5. Create

Creative talent can be highly variable, but when it works, it can generate high quality for little or no cost.

The one-sentence summary

You are what you share, so start with a core idea and get others to contribute, collaborate and create.

That's the essence of the book. It is not set out in any particular sections. It is more like a very long essay. As such it is not easy to dip in and out, nor to refer back to something in particular. That, one assumes, is the very nature of co-creation via 258 authors. What you gain in a vast melting pot of ideas and suggestions, you may lose in the workload of trying to edit them down to something manageable that suits your needs. So it is best to treat it as a thought-provoking whole, rather than anything specific you can take action on. If you are happy to let things take their course, then this approach may be for you, but if you are something of a control freak, it may well give you the heebie-jeebies.

CHAPTER 5 WISDOM

- Play is the fermenting ground for exploring alternatives and as such is the very essence of creativity.

- There is no point in pursuing creativity without a purpose.

- When considering creative ideas, concentrate on the size of the idea, not the size of the budget.

- It is possible to codify the rules that make a great idea, but equally you might want to ignore them all in search of originality.

- You can be more creative if you train yourself to think differently.

- You are what you share, so start with a core idea and get others to contribute, collaborate and create.

"I need you to fire Sandra Rownbotham. I'd do it if I wasn't sleeping with her."

CHAPTER 6. PERSONAL ORGANISATION: HOW TO GET ON WITH IT

Keep it simple

The Laws of Simplicity JOHN MAEDA

After our rapid canter through the world of marketing and all the expert advice that can be heeded, we arrive at the action part. Marketers can draw as many diagrams as they like, talk endlessly, disappear for days in strategy away-days, write the most lucid briefs ever, but it all amounts to nothing unless they get on and do something. Customers do not utter in astonishment: *'What a great campaign! I wonder how many meetings they had to create that?'*

So in this last chapter we concentrate on how on earth you can get all this thinking applied to your business effectively. It is all down to how you organise things. Keep it simple, says John Maeda in *The Laws of Simplicity*, first published in 2006. Simplicity equals sanity, he says, and outlines 10 laws:

1. **Reduce**

   The simplest way to achieve simplicity is through thoughtful reduction.

2. **Organise**

   Organisation makes a system of many appear fewer.

3. **Time**

   Savings in time feel like simplicity.

4. **Learn**

   Knowledge makes everything simpler.

5. **Differences**

   Simplicity and complexity need each other.

6. **Context**
   What lies in the periphery of simplicity is definitely not peripheral.

7. **Emotion**
   More emotions are better than fewer.

8. **Trust**
   In simplicity we trust.

9. **Failure**
   Some things can never be made simple.

10. **The One**
    Simplicity is about subtracting the obvious, and adding the meaningful.

If that seems a pretty clinical list, then get used to it. When you want to get something done, brevity is everything. Indeed, there are many who believe that brevity equals intelligence, so the shorter you can make something, the better thought through it is likely to be. The book is short, which it should be. It has a number of systems for reducing the complex down to simpler thinking. There are three keys to this:

- *Away* – more appears like less by simply moving it far away from its original point

- *Open* – openness simplifies complexity

- *Power* – use less, gain more

Again, the starkness of the simple can be frightening. Stare at his suggestions until you have read something helpful in them. As Einstein said: *'Everything should be made as simple as possible, but no simpler.'* He offers plenty of ways to sort out complex things. Consider the alternatives here:

How simple can you make it? v. How complex does it have to be?

How can you make the wait shorter? v. How can you make the wait more tolerable?

The author has a preoccupation with technology, and is a fan of acronyms to help remember organisational systems. For example:

- **SHE: Shrink, Hide, Embody**

- **SLIP: Sort, Label, Integrate, Prioritise**

- **BRAIN: Basics, Repeat, Avoid (desperation), Inspire, Never (forget to repeat)**

The one-sentence summary
Simplicity equals sanity, so make everything as simple as possible, but no simpler.

In honour of the spirit of this section, that's all I am going to say on the matter.

Articulate yourself well

High Impact Speeches RICHARD HELLER
You can't talk straight if you can't think straight, and vice versa. A vast proportion of the difficulties that marketers encounter are centred on poor expression and lack of

clarity. The fact that much of this confusion is generated by those who are supposed to be experts in communication has caused more than a few ironic smiles in the business world. People need to articulate themselves well, whether in writing or using speech, says Richard Heller in *High Impact Speeches.* Subtitled *How to Create and Deliver Words that Move Minds,* the book tells you how to deal with the request to make a speech – whether to accept the invitation, what to research, and how to get the response you want. But it does a lot more than that, because it runs through all the disciplines required to form a decent line of argument. This is crucial stuff given the very high propensity of people these days to start talking before they have worked out what they are going to say.

The right structure and preparation are essential, as are researching your audience, several edits, and proper rehearsal. If you want to speak well, you need to know how to write, and vice versa. There are three basic principles for good speech making:

- **Speak the truth;**

- **Listen for the truth;**

- **Be true to yourself.**

These would be good principles for life, let alone speech making. If everybody did this every day in business, companies would be far more successful. Anyway, enough of the pipe dreaming – it's never going to happen. The book contains lots of good advice, and if you are anxious about making a speech, it guides you through the whole process:

1. **Do I have to?**
   Work out when to accept an invitation to speak.

2. **What you must research**
   Knowledge of the venue and audience is critical.

3. **I came here for a result**
   You need to work out what impact you wish to have.

4. **Speech architecture**
   The right structure needs careful planning. All speeches are essentially the same in architecture.

5. **Write it down and talk it out**
   Writing and talking are not the same thing, so work out the differences.

6. **Don't be patronising**
   The moment you condescend your audience, you will have lost them, and you won't achieve your objective.

7. **Killer facts**
   These can come as single shots or sustained salvoes.

8. **Beware of negative arguments**
   They make you sound negative, which is perilously close to being unpleasant.

9. **Rehearsal is crucial**
   It is an endless process of discovery, so you learn a lot about yourself as well as improving your performance.

10. **Judicious silence**
    This is very powerful and often has a mesmeric effect on an audience.

He then runs through a series of tricks and techniques to add clarity, colour, rhythm, pace, emotion and persuasion. You need to take some trouble to choose an accurate title, and be aware that some speeches do not so much peter out but simply drop dead. A speech is a very concentrated form of conversation, and almost every great speech changes pace several times. No one really likes a guest who domineers or rants or shouts, so that should be avoided at all costs.

The one-sentence summary
Before you say something, work out what you are going to say.

Of course you can't just suddenly become a great speaker so, although this book provides a framework, it is no substitute for having an idea and a point of view. There are summaries at the end of each chapter to enable you to short-circuit everything, and some extracts from great speeches. But you will have to put the bulk of the work in yourself. It is a superb discipline to sit down with a blank piece of paper and quietly work out what on earth you wish to say. It doesn't matter in what medium your line of argument is to be delivered – it is imperative that you know what you are going to say, and why. All good marketers need to communicate effectively with both the written and spoken word, but the suspicion is that these days not enough attention is paid to the communication of either.

Present your company or brand well

How Not to Come Second DAVID KEAN
Perfect Pitch JON STEEL
Presenting your company or brand well is crucial. Now we look at the art of pitching and presenting an argument with

How Not to Come Second by David Kean, and *Perfect Pitch* by Jon Steel. *How Not to Come Second,* first published in 2006, is subtitled *The Art of Winning Business Pitches.* It returns frequently to the point that it is all about the winning. Far too many pitches fail because people don't do the simple things and get distracted. Now we don't want to turn this into a macho competition, so let's just work on the principle that you will usually wish to prevail with your view, or per-suade someone of the merits of your line of argument. This could be a customer, a boss or a colleague. The basics of good organisation, having a persuasive manner and getting things done as a result are all crucial.

The ingredients for successful pitching are:

- *be organised*;

- *know your audience* (many pitch blind);

- *solve the problem*;

- *price properly* (note: not 'cheaply');

- *practice* (methodically, not at the last minute);

- *great presentations*;

- *unstoppable momentum*;

- *feedback.*

Other advice includes compiling the pitch bible, meeting every day, brainstorming with the top talent, networking like crazy, and having a mole on the other side. If you are working in a team, it identifies four types (expressives, ami-ables, drivers, analyticals) who may be present on either side. They require careful consideration and a good match-ing of characters.

Pitch on a postcard is a good idea – if you can't fit your argument on one, it's probably not good enough. Elements of getting it wrong include deluding yourself that you were a very close second, trying to over-complicate things that are actually simple and people who are professionals most of the time but who act like amateurs in the pitch process. Do you recognise any of these qualities in presentations in your company? Those whom you wish to persuade will most likely be looking for good team dynamics, people who understand them and their business, some fun and stimulation, good value, and problem solving. There is many a presentation that does not deliver any of these at all.

The one-sentence summary
Present something ingenious, express it simply, stick to the point, and solve the problem.

Perfect Pitch, from 2007, says that most business presentations could and should be much better than they are. It identifies a range of presentation crimes committed every day in business, and the pillars on which successful presentations are built. The importance of listening and understanding audience psychology are stressed as vital, as is the rehearsal, the preparation, the leave-behind and the approach after the pitch, which are frequently more important than the pitch itself. There is a lot of experience here in anecdote from 20 years in advertising, all of which is underpinned by the point that the presentation doesn't actually have to be perfect – just better than any other competing company or view. There is a five-step programme to be followed:

1. Grazing
Data dump and gather raw materials.

2. Looking for meaning
Establish connections and write down all possible ideas.

3. Drop it
Take a break, get away from the problem, and view it afresh later.

4. Adapt and distil
Make the ideas make sense to anybody, and ensure simplicity.

5. Writing the presentation
Don't lecture – communicate, remember that bullet points dilute thought, and that clip art is a way of saying you have no imagination.

The book is subtitled *The Art of Selling Ideas and Winning New Business*. You may not specifically be in the business of winning new business, but everybody has to sell their ideas. It is heavy on anecdote, but not on method, so don't expect a step-by-step guide. My favourite story concerns the thought that the more connected we are, the less intelligent we become, in which the author ceremoniously runs over his BlackBerry with his Porsche, but it still works so he has to use his neighbour's sledgehammer to finish the job.

Unless you can present your company or brand well, you are unlikely to be a successful marketer. The knack is to pay great attention to straightforward things: think hard, generate clever ideas, express them simply and don't patronise your audience. This approach will work almost every time.

Are you the right person to do it?

The E-Myth Revisited MICHAEL E. GERBER

Occasionally you may find that if you have trouble getting on with something, it is because you are actually not the right person to do it. There is a knack to working this out that is well articulated by Michael E. Gerber in *The E-Myth Revisited*, first published in 1995. The book is based on the assertion that most small businesses don't work, and explains what they can do about it. Although it is predominantly about small businesses, there is much here that big businesses can learn. Indeed, there are many who believe that all corporation staff should have a stint at running their own business, precisely so that they do not lose touch with the real world. Marketers in particular are often accused of transmitting messages from an ivory tower.

Gerber believes that there are two big myths about people who start their own businesses:

1. **Most are entrepreneurs**
   In fact, they probably aren't.

2. **An individual who understands the technical work of a business can successfully run a business that does that technical work**
   This assumption is usually wrong and can be fatal to the business.

He defines this as The Fatal Assumption: that if you understand the technical work of a business, then you understand the business that does that technical work. In fact, those running businesses need to be part entrepreneur, part manager, and part technician. If they can't, then they need others to perform these roles. The first frame of mind thinks ahead and dreams, the second controls and restrains, the third gets the work done. Businesses move from infancy (the technician's phase), to adolescence (getting some help), to going beyond the comfort zone to eventual maturity. The relevance of all this to marketers is that, if you have difficulty doing something, you may not actually be the right person to do the job.

This point may not apply to your entire job, but it probably does to aspects of it. An ability to distinguish between tasks that you are good or bad at could be crucial to how you organise yourself and, ultimately, whether or not important things get done. If the task is that important, then it shouldn't really matter who does it, so long as it gets done well and in time. *'Contrary to popular belief, my experience has shown me that the people who are exceptionally good in business aren't so because of what they know but because of their insatiable need to know more.'*

The idea of *an Entrepreneurial Seizure* is a good one. One day you suddenly ask *Why am I doing this?* and start imagining your own business because you are so fed up with the sluggish way your corporation does things. In this respect, the author is drawing a direct link between ideas and action:

'The difference between creativity and innovation is the difference between thinking about getting things done in the world and getting things done.'

The one-sentence summary
If you want to get something done, first work out if you are the best person to do it.

There are whole books on personal organisation and how to get things done, but this isn't one of them. It's all about self-realisation. If you need to get something done, consider whether you are the best person for the job. If not, find a colleague who can do it, or do it better. If you absolutely have to do it yourself, then you will need to develop a system.

You need a system

Simply Brilliant FERGUS O'CONNELL

Really what it all boils down to is that you need a system to get anything done at all, says Fergus O'Connell in *Simply Brilliant* (2001). Things either are or they aren't, so stop making excuses and get on with it. Sound advice indeed. Too many marketing ideas have been consigned to history through inertia. He believes that the best ideas aren't always complicated and the incredibly straightforward stuff is often overlooked in the search for a complex answer. Many smart people lack the set of essential skills that could roughly be described as 'common sense'. He outlines seven principles that can be adapted for attacking most everyday problems:

1. **Many things are simple**
   This is despite our tendency to complicate them.

2. **You need to know what you're trying to do**
   Amazingly, many people don't.

3. **There is always a sequence of events**
   Make the journey in your head before you start.

4. **Things don't get done if people don't do them**
   Strategic wafflers beware, as we saw in previous chapters.

5. **Things rarely turn out as expected**
   So plan for the unexpected.

6. **Things either are or they aren't**
   Don't fudge things.

7. **Look at things from other's point of view**
   It will help your expectations.

In a world of over-complication, asking some simple questions can really make your life easier. Some people love to make things more complicated than they really are, but there truly is no need. For example, try these ideas:

What would be the simplest thing to do here?

Describe an issue or a solution in less than 25 words

Tell it as though you were telling a six year old

Ask whether there is a simpler way

Try writing the minutes of a meeting before the meeting – then you'll know what you want to get out of it. The book highlights the difference between duration and effort. *'How long will it take you to have a look at that?' 'About an hour.'* But when? It explains the reasons why things don't get done: confusion, over-commitment, inability – usually busy people never say there's a problem. So you need to plan your time assuming you will have interruptions – the *'hot date'* scenario, whereby you always manage to leave the office if you have one.

The one-sentence summary
Life is simpler than you think, so get on with it.

The orientation of the book draws heavily from the project management perspective, which is a rigorous discipline worth trying to imitate. You will probably want to cherry-pick the most applicable ideas that suit you best, as I have done here. Anyone who flies by the seat of their pants would have to be very disciplined to apply them. It's a bit like dieting, but it really works.

CHAPTER 6 WISDOM

- **Simplicity equals sanity, so make everything as simple as possible, but no simpler.**

- **Before you say something, work out what you are going to say.**

- **Present something ingenious, express it simply, stick to the point, and solve the problem.**

- **If you want to get something done, first work out if you are the best person to do it.**

- **Life is simpler than you think, so get on with it.**

APPENDIX I:
A NEW
MARKETING
MANIFESTO

35 points that might help marketers

THE BIG THEMES

- Ignore what you have done before, decide on something distinctive to do, and do that one thing with full commitment

- To make corporations change effectively, the people who work in them have to behave differently, or be told how to do so

- Endless choice is creating unlimited demand so you probably need to re-think your business model: make everything available and help customers find it easily (online)

- The customers that your data says are your most satisfied may be the most likely to leave tomorrow, so are you asking the right questions and measuring the right dimensions?

- Most news stories are planted by PR agencies without verification and cannot be believed – everybody knows this, so the whole system is discredited

- Marketing is a mess, so stop over-complicating everything and do some simple thinking based on your brand's obvious differentiating characteristics

MARKETING

- Marketing acts as a bridge between an organisation and the outside world, and is central to every company, but it doesn't have to be wrapped up in complicated jargon that confuses everyone

- When you start looking at exactly how much things cost and how much profit you are making you become a much better marketer

- Brands are the new traditions, increasingly playing the role that tradition used to play by giving people ideas to live by

- Human relationships are fundamental to successful advertising communication, and good research should be a catalyst for great creative ideas, not an obstacle to them

- Everything you do or don't do, or say or don't say, communicates something about your brand

- It is the end of business as usual because online conversations have changed forever the way companies need to interact with their customers, so one-way rhetoric from head office simply doesn't wash

BRANDS AND BRANDING

- Brands and branding must be grounded in a rigorous and philosophical view of the way the world works

- Customer perception of brand quality is a combination of pre-existing expectations and experience when interacting with it, so companies need to practise what they preach

- All organisations must behave impeccably and manage their public relations with intelligence if they are to safeguard their reputation

- Generating word of mouth is the cheapest way to generate brand publicity, but you have to get it started

- Creating loyalty beyond reason requires emotional connections that generate the highest levels of love and respect for your brand

- Build your brand, redefine the market and defy convention by generating a brand molecule instead of an old-fashioned unique selling point

CONSUMER BEHAVIOUR

- People do some very strange things, so don't take anything for granted

- There will always be someone who wishes to generate fear and panic, but they are usually biased, ill-informed or just plain wrong

- Most middle class people have too much of everything, but it hasn't made them any happier

- Forget individual choice – people just copy each other, but crowds usually get it right

- Trust your first instinct, because a snap judgement can actually be far more effective than one you make deliberately and cautiously

- One imaginative person applying a well-placed lever can move the world

CREATIVITY

- Play is the fermenting ground for exploring alternatives and as such is the very essence of creativity

- There is no point in pursuing creativity without a purpose

- When considering creative ideas, concentrate on the size of the idea, not the size of the budget

- It is possible to codify the rules that make a great idea, but equally you might want to ignore them all in search of originality

- You can be more creative if you train yourself to think differently

- You are what you share, so start with a core idea and get others to contribute, collaborate and create

PERSONAL ORGANISATION: HOW TO GET ON WITH IT

- Simplicity equals sanity, so make everything as simple as possible, but no simpler

- Before you say something, work out what you are going to say

- Present something ingenious, express it simply, stick to the point, and solve the problem

- If you want to get something done, first work out if you are the best person to do the job

- Life is simpler than you think, so get on with it

APPENDIX II:
THE ONE-MINUTE
SUMMARIES

Affluenza OLIVER JAMES

WHAT THE BOOK SAYS
- This is not a book about communications but it provides deep insights into the psychology of humans and as such is important for consumer understanding.
- Affluenza is defined as a contagious middle-class virus causing depression, addiction and ennui. This is an epidemic sweeping the world.
- In order to counteract it and ensure our mental health, we should pursue our needs rather than our wants – the majority of which are unsustainable.
- There is a questionnaire at the beginning to establish whether you have the virus, and a manifesto at the end suggesting how it can be stopped.

WHAT'S GOOD ABOUT IT
- There are hundreds of examples from all over the world and sources from academic studies to demonstrate that this is not simply a biased rant
- The author outlines many possible vaccines to the virus, which include:
  - *Have positive volition* (not Think Positive) – make choices
  - *Replace virus motives* (with intrinsic ones) – for the right reasons
  - *Be beautiful* (not attractive) – don't conform to a marketing ideal
  - *Consume what you need* (not what advertisers want *you to want*)
  - *Meet your children's needs* (not those of little adults)
  - *Educate your children* (don't brainwash them)
  - *Enjoy motherhood* (not desperate housewifery/ househusbandry)
  - *Be authentic* (not sincere), *vivacious* (not hyperactive) and *playful* (not game-playing)
- In addition you need to sort out your childhood and reject much of the status quo in order to be a satisfied, unstressed individual.

WHAT YOU HAVE TO WATCH

- It contains a pretty blistering condemnation of the advertising industry and goes so far as to recommend a total ban on exceptionally attractive models.
- Because the author is a psychologist, he is prone to recommending therapy, which may not suit everybody. Willpower could be just as effective.

Blink   MALCOLM GLADWELL

WHAT THE BOOK SAYS

- Our ability to 'know' something in a split-second judgement, without really knowing why we know, is one of the most powerful abilities we possess.
- A snap judgement can actually be far more effective than one we make deliberately and cautiously.
- By blocking out what is irrelevant and focusing on narrow slices of experience, we can read seemingly complex situations in the blink of eye.
- This is essentially 'thinking without thinking.
- He introduces the theory of 'thin slicing' – using the first two seconds of any encounter to determine intuitively your response or the likely outcome.
- He demonstrates that this 'little bit of knowledge' can go a long way, and is accurate in over 80 per cent of instances.

WHAT'S GOOD ABOUT IT

- There are scores of vivid examples in which peoples' first instincts have been right, but they cannot explain why. These include an art dealer identifying a fake statue that the Getty museum believes to be genuine, a tennis coach being able to predict every time when players are about to serve a double fault, and a psychologist accurately guessing years in advance if married couples will stay together or not.

- The thinking is a welcome counterpoint to a world in which too much reliance on proof and data has replaced hunch and instinct.
- The value of spontaneity is highlighted by the example of a forces commander who comprehensively beats better-equipped opposition in a US military exercise because he consistently does the opposite of what the computers predict.
- He goes on to show that, strangely, it is possible to give 'structure' to spontaneity, by consciously going against the grain in order to generate an outcome that is surprising to the other party, but not to you.

WHAT YOU HAVE TO WATCH

- Although the subject matter is fascinating, there are so many experts interviewed that the average reader would not be able to enact any of the skills necessary to take advantage of the findings, other than the basic point that you should trust your first instincts more.

Brand Manners   PRINGLE & GORDON

WHAT THE BOOK SAYS

- Companies need to align their internal and external brand values to build a self-confident organisation.
- Customer perception of quality is a function of their pre-existing expectations of the brand, coupled with their experience when interacting with it.
- Brand reputations can be ruined by a poor interaction.
- The Brand Manners Improvement Cycle has five stages:

  1. *Individual Behaviours*. It's not enough to talk about missions and values – they have to be manifested in the concrete reality of individual actions

  2. *Encounters*. Stay close to customers and staff, and engender an atmosphere of trust

3. *Brand Promise.* **Technology and automation must not be allowed to remove humanity from brand interaction**

4. *Happy Surprises.* **Direct human interface generates defining gestures, pledges to customers, and moments of truth that should reflect the brand**

5. *Feeling Good.* **The art of ensuring continually satisfied customers is to define your version of outstanding service, realise the importance of under-promising and over-delivering, and recruit in line with the brand's values**

WHAT'S GOOD ABOUT IT

- **The Brand Manners cycle makes good sense and enables you to start a strategic debate that goes way beyond marketing communications.**
- **The philosophy of the book is a useful antidote to macho marketing styles.**
- **Case histories include Orange, Tesco, Coca-Cola, Ronseal, HSBC, and Pret A Manger – many of which could be directly applicable to your business.**
- **The format is in user-friendly chunks, with lots of diagrams that may help to inspire the content of other presentations.**

WHAT YOU HAVE TO WATCH

- **Face-to-face interaction with customers may be one step too far removed from the briefs for most marketing campaigns.**
- **You could end up having a lot of theoretical debate about the behaviour in an organisation without making any particular progress on marketing issues.**

Buzz   SALZMAN, MATATHIA & O'REILLY

WHAT THE BOOK SAYS

- **Everyone has a different definition of buzz, but roughly it has to be organic, centred on conversational value, peer** driven, and spread outwards from trend setters to trend spreaders and on to the mainstream.

- The only thing consumers trust these days is personal experience.
- Word of mouth (WOM) should be renamed WORM (Word of Relevant Mouth) because of the way it insinuates itself into the conscious.
- There is a Buzz Continuum which runs from the lunatic fringe (2 per cent), to the Alphas (8 per cent), to the Bees (20 per cent), to the mainstream (50 per cent), to the laggards (20 per cent).
- Much of buzz marketing lies in the critical zone between 'best kept secret' and 'everyone's doing it'.

WHAT'S GOOD ABOUT IT

- It is probably worth trying to explain and categorise a phenomenon which plays a large part in modern marketing but is quite hard to describe.
- Media saturation is nicely summarised: 'a single weekday edition of the *New York Times* contains more data than a typical c.17 citizen of England would have encountered in a lifetime'.
- It acknowledges the similarity to *The Tipping Point* and tries to build on it by explaining the role of superconnectors and by adding a degree of quantification and case history work to the concept.
- It offers four springboards to generate buzz:
  - *cultivate a culture of creativity;*
  - *give 'em (consumers) what they always wanted;*
  - *capture the moment;*
  - *challenge the conventions.*
- It is honest enough to include advice on how to handle negative buzz as well as generate the positive – a form of crisis management.

WHAT YOU HAVE TO WATCH

- The thinking is not particularly original. It is very much a reorganisation of lots of other recent work that covers

influencers, tipping points, and how to seed trends in influential minorities in order to ignite mass acceptance.
- It is written by people who work for Euro RSCG, so it is rather self-congratulatory and from time to time strays into the realm of credentials.

Commitment-led Marketing JAN HOFMEYR & BUTCH RICE

WHAT THE BOOK SAYS
- The key to brand profits is in the customer's mind.
- Some customers appear to be loyal because they habitually buy a product, but this does not mean they are committed to it.
- The Conversion Model allows you to segment users by commitment to stay, and non-users by openness to adopt your brand.
- By applying this to your brand, and competitors, you can identify the right strategy to defend share (if you are a large brand), or steal it (if small).
- Customer satisfaction is a poor predictor of behaviour – commitment is better.
- Loyalty is what customers do; commitment is what they feel.
- Customers can appear deceptively loyal but actually be uncommitted (they might only use the brand because everyone else does (Microsoft), through lack of choice, affordability, or distribution.

WHAT'S GOOD ABOUT IT
- There is a useful segmentation element: Users are entrenched or average (committed); shallow or convertible (uncommitted). Non-users are available or ambivalent (open); weakly or strongly (unavailable).
- Few clients correctly measure these features for all the brands in their market – if they did, they could make better-informed decisions.

- The idea that 'satisfied' customers may be very prepared to leave your brand is clever. Is your client measuring the wrong attribute? Can they identify a competitor's Achilles heel?
- A 'last straw' can make a committed user snap and switch to another. The moment is hard to predict, the decision is usually irreversible, and to cap it all they tend to become a missionary *against* that brand. Clients beware!
- There is a level-headed, unbiased review of how advertising works.
- There is an amusing example showing the correlation between the number of lamp-posts in the world and the number of babies born every year, which shows the danger of assuming causality between variables.

WHAT YOU HAVE TO WATCH
- There are quite a few examples from politics and religion whose relevance to conventional marketing is a bit tenuous.
- In order to benefit from the thinking in the book, you would have to endorse it completely, invest heavily in implementing what it proposes and be very patient whilst the data become apparent.

Eating the Big Fish   ADAM MORGAN

WHAT THE BOOK SAYS
- Most marketing books are written about brand leaders, but most marketing people don't work on leading brands.
- These challenger brands need to behave differently if they are to compete with brand leaders – effectively doing more with less.
- There are eight credos:
  1. *Break with your immediate past* (forget everything you know and think again)
  2. *Build a lighthouse identity* (state what you are – don't reflect consumers)

3. *Assume thought leadership of category* (the one everyone talks about)
4. *Create symbols of re-evaluation* (do the unexpected)
5. *Sacrifice* (work out what you are not going to do)
6. *Over-commitment* (karate experts aim two feet below the brick to break it)
7. *Use advertising/publicity to enter popular culture*
8. *Become ideas-centred, not consumer-centred* (constantly re-invent)

WHAT'S GOOD ABOUT IT
- It concentrates on practical things that most brands can do.
- It tells you how to run a workshop and apply the thinking.
- Most of the credos can be used to overcome inertia.
- It can help small, under-resourced marketing teams to mobilise big ideas.
- Brand leaders can benefit from thinking like a challenger to stay number one.

WHAT YOU HAVE TO WATCH
- It is easy to go round talking about 'creating a lighthouse identity' (and other phrases) without actually saying anything.
- Some of the ideas are easier said than done.
- Credo number seven is easy to criticise because you would expect a communications expert to recommend activity.

Enough   JOHN NAISH

WHAT THE BOOK SAYS
- Our basic survival strategy makes us chase more of everything: status, food, information, possessions. Now, thanks to technology, we've suddenly got more of everything than we can ever use.
- We urgently need to develop a sense of 'enough', and an ability to enjoy what we have, rather than a fixation with 'more'.

- On the data and information front, we are suffering from *infobesity*. Too much information causes stress and confusion and makes us do irrational things.
- Twenty-four-hour news media suffers from an *'Elvis still dead'* syndrome that distorts our view of the world to the point that we have forgotten what true news is.
- A personal data diet creates time for proper thought and interaction.
- Purchasing items gives us a dopamine rush but it wears off almost immediately. Thousands of women routinely return everything on a Monday that they bought on Saturday. Retailers call them *shoe-limics*.

WHAT'S GOOD ABOUT IT

- The concept of *presenteeism* is interesting. This is where people spend hours at their desks not achieving anything because they are too tired, stressed, under-stimulated, distracted or depressed to be productive.
- Workaholics Anonymous is a new movement based on AA principles. In an extreme paradox, earning more simply increases discontentment.
- If you don't know what 'enough' is, you are not free.
- Corporate Stockholm Syndrome makes people believe that their overwork habits are driven by irresistible external forces. They then frown on normal timekeepers and make their lives a misery.
- *'All the gear but no idea'* applies to fair-weather sports enthusiasts but could equally be applied to many who cannot stop stockpiling possessions.
- We have too many options – a torture of choice. Sixty per cent of adults only use half of the functions on their devices. Only one in six reads the manual.
- WILFing is a pointless form of shopping: *What Was I Looking For?*
- We always think things will be better in the future. Present quality of life is deemed to be 6.9 out of 10 (and guessed at 8.2 in 5 years' time). But when the time comes, it's still 6.9.

WHAT YOU HAVE TO WATCH
- Not much. Towards the end the message becomes somewhat environmental and a little bit preachy, but this is more than offset by the great research and interesting angles in the main part.

Flat Earth News   NICK DAVIES
WHAT THE BOOK SAYS
- Global media is full of falsehood, distortion and propaganda.
- The author is a journalist who started investigating his own colleagues, only to discover that the business of reporting the truth had been slowly subverted by the mass production of ignorance.
- Among the culprits are the Sunday paper that allows MI6 and the CIA to plant fiction in its columns; a newsroom that routinely rejects stories about black people and papers that support law and order but pay cash bribes to bent detectives.
- Many stories are no more accurate than claiming the earth is flat, including the Millennium Bug and WMD in Iraq. These taint government policy and pervert belief.
- Most reporters do not have time to check what they are sent – instead they rely on the Press Association or PR stories to generate 'churnalism'.
- His research shows that 70 per cent of stories are wholly or partly rewritten from wire copy, without further corroboration.
- The rules of production are dictated by the media moguls: cut costs by running cheap stories, selecting safe facts and ideas, avoiding the electric fence (any bodies that can hurt the press) and always giving both sides of the story.
- Increase revenue by giving the readers what they want to believe in.

WHAT'S GOOD ABOUT IT
- It's a very ballsy, well-researched book, as you would expect from an investigative journalist.
- Revisiting the cosy relationship between PR and the media can't be a bad thing.

WHAT YOU HAVE TO WATCH
- Public Relations and newspapers are up in arms about the book.
- It names names, in a specific and authoritative way.
- There is a tinge of 'chip on shoulder' about it.
- If you work in PR, you need some decent answers to the allegations.

Flicking Your Creative Switch PEASE & LOTHERINGTON

WHAT THE BOOK SAYS
- Everyone can be creative, regardless of whether they think they are.
- Creativity is variously described as 'the spark that ignites new ideas', 'the infinite capacity that resides within you', and 'shaping the game you play, not playing the game you find'.
- Good ideas arise when we take something we already know (light bulb number one) and consider it in relation to another thing we already know but which is unrelated (light bulb number two). Merging them creates light bulb number three – the new idea.

WHAT'S GOOD ABOUT IT
- It explains the origin of the phrase 'thinking outside the box'. The Gottschaldt figurine, or nine-dot game, requires you to join all the dots without taking your pen off the paper. You can't solve it if you view it as a box.
- ROI is used to stand for Relevance, Originality and Impact. Your ideas won't work if they do not have all three.

- Barriers to creativity have been placed in our way since childhood: *don't be foolish, grow up, work before play, do as you're told, don't ask questions, obey the rules, be practical* and so on.
- There are six techniques which you can use in any away-day to generate ideas:
  - *Random Word:* take a noun randomly from somewhere and apply it to the subject. You can also use pictures.
  - *Eyes of Experts:* choose three respected experts from other fields and consider how they would deal with your issue. There is a variation called Industrial Roundabout where you view it through a different category.
  - *What's Hot?:* use popular current things to appeal to your audience.
  - *Curly Questions:* use analogies, speculation, role reversal and imagination to re-phrase the issue at hand so that more original answers emerge.
  - *Exaggeration and Depravation:* over-exaggerate the benefits of a product, or push to ludicrous extremes what happens if that product isn't present.
  - *Exquisite Corpse:* based on surrealist thinking, different people randomly select five words to create a sentence in the pattern adjective/noun/verb/adjective/noun. E.g. *The peculiar bicycle swims a brilliant banana.* Each word is then scrutinised to review the problem.

WHAT YOU HAVE TO WATCH
- You need to control the exercises so they don't seem trivial.
- You need an open mind.

Herd   MARK EARLS

WHAT THE BOOK SAYS
- It is subtitled *How to Change Mass Behaviour by Harnessing our True Nature.*

- The main point is that, whilst marketers are banging on about individual choice and one-to-one marketing, in fact everybody just copies, or is influenced by, other people.
- As such, most attempts by marketers to alter mass behaviour fail because they are based on a false premise.
- This is why most government initiatives struggle to create real change, why so much marketing money fails to drive sales, why M&A programmes actually *reduce* shareholder value and most internal change projects don't deliver any lasting transformation.

WHAT'S GOOD ABOUT IT

- It explains the 'why' of our struggles to influence mass behaviour.
- Most of us in the West have misunderstood the mechanics ('the how') of mass behaviour because we have misplaced notions of what it means to be human.
- There is a huge range of diverse anecdotes and evidence – from Peter Kay and urinal etiquette to international rugby and the rise of the Arctic Monkeys – to show that we are, at heart, a 'we' species, but one suffering from the 'illusion of I'.
- It challenges most standard conceptions about marketing and forces the reader to rethink the whole thing.
- The seven principles of Herd marketing are:
  - ☐ *Interaction* (between people)
  - ☐ *Influence* (of certain people)
  - ☐ *Us-Talk* (the power of word of mouth)
  - ☐ *Just Believe* (stand for something and stick to it)
  - ☐ *(Re-)Light the fire* (overcoming cynicism by restating the original idea)
  - ☐ *Co-creativity* (let others join in)
  - ☐ *Letting go* (you never were in charge of your brand)

WHAT YOU HAVE TO WATCH

- Nothing: it's great.

High Impact Speeches RICHARD HELLER

WHAT THE BOOK SAYS

- It tells you how to deal with the request to make a speech – whether to accept the invitation, what to research and how to get the response you want.
- The right structure and preparation are essential, as are researching your audience, several edits and proper rehearsal.
- If you want to speak well, you need to know how to write, and vice versa.
- There are three basic principles for good speech making: speak the truth, listen for the truth, and be true to yourself.

WHAT'S GOOD ABOUT IT

- The book contains lots of good advice, and if you are anxious about making a speech, it guides you through the whole process.
- It is full of good quotes such as:
  - □ *It is significant that 'dumb' has come to mean not only silent but stupid*
  - □ *Don't be patronising*
  - □ *Take some trouble to choose an accurate title*
  - □ *All speeches are essentially the same in architecture*
  - □ *Some speeches do not peter out but simply drop dead*
  - □ *A speech is a very concentrated form of conversation*
  - □ *Almost every great speech changes pace several times*
  - □ *No one likes a guest who domineers or rants or shouts*
  - □ *Using negative arguments makes you sound negative, which is perilously close to being unpleasant*
  - □ *Killer facts can come as shots or salvoes*
  - □ *Rehearsal is an endless process of discovery*
  - □ *Judicious silence has a mesmeric effect on an audience*
- There are summaries at the end of each chapter to enable you to short-circuit everything.
- Some extracts from great speeches are included.

WHAT YOU HAVE TO WATCH
- You can't just suddenly become a great speaker so, although this book provides a framework, it is no substitute for having an idea and a point of view.

How Not To Come Second   DAVID KEAN

WHAT THE BOOK SAYS
- This book is subtitled *The Art of Winning Business Pitches*.
- The author used to work at Lowe, DDB, and Omnicom.
- It constantly returns to the point that it is all about the winning. Far too many pitches fail because people don't do the simple things and get distracted.
- Elements of getting it wrong include: deluding yourself that you were a very close second; trying to over complicate things that are actually simple; and people who are professionals most of the time acting like amateurs in the pitch process.

WHAT'S GOOD ABOUT IT
- Although it's all obvious stuff, clients want a good team, people who understand them and their business, some fun and stimulation, good value, and problem solving. There is many a pitch that does not deliver these.
- The ingredients for successful pitching are:
  - □ be organised;
  - □ know your audience (many agencies pitch blind);
  - □ solve the problem;
  - □ price properly (note – not 'cheaply');
  - □ practise (methodically, not at the last minute);
  - □ great presentations;
  - □ unstoppable momentum;
  - □ feedback.
- Other advice includes compiling the pitch bible, meeting every day, brainstorming with the top talent, networking like crazy and having a mole on the client side.

- It identifies four types (expressives, amiables, drivers, analyticals) who may be present on your team and the client side. They require careful casting.
- Pitch on a postcard is a good idea – if you can't fit your argument on one, it's not good enough.

WHAT YOU HAVE TO WATCH
- The author is English but the book has been adapted for an American audience.
- It briefly falls back on De Bono's Six-Hat Thinking, which isn't new.

In Search of The Obvious   JACK TROUT

WHAT THE BOOK SAYS
- Subtitled *The Antidote for Today's Marketing Mess*, this is a pointed polemic about the state that marketing has got itself into. He gives a thorough pasting to marketing, advertising, research, Wall Street, the Internet and several named client companies.
- Instead of concentrating on segmentation, customer retention or search engine optimisation, marketers should be looking for that simple, obvious and differentiating idea.
- Particular culprits are people and organisations that deliberately put complication in the way of the obvious – and shoot themselves in the foot.
- Many people fear the activity of thinking so they follow suggestions made by others to avoid it.

WHAT'S GOOD ABOUT IT
- We seem to have no time to think any more. Many meetings are little more than gadget envy sessions.
- *'The art of being wise is the art of knowing what to overlook.'* William James.
- Mission statements are denounced as bunk. A survey of 300 revealed that the words used in them are all the same: service (230), customers (211), quality (194), value, employees, growth, environment, profit, leader and best.

- Sales, technology and performance leadership are all valid concepts. Thought leadership is not – it doesn't mean anything.
- If you want to solve a problem, try: substitute, combine, adapt, magnify, minimise, eliminate and a range of other angular thinking techniques.
- The biggest blunders these days are: Me-too products or ideas, being unclear what you are selling, untruthful claims and arrogance brought on by success.

WHAT YOU HAVE TO WATCH
- All the examples are American, so you have to work with them.
- He has quite a rant. There are moments when the vitriol appears to outweigh rational analysis, but some may find that fun.

Juicing The Orange   FALLON & SENN

WHAT THE BOOK SAYS
- It is subtitled *How to Turn Creativity into a Powerful Business Advantage.*
- Most leaders have more creativity in their organisations than they realise.
- Identify one critical business problem that needs solving and then rigorously unearth insights that lead to a spectacular solution.
- There are Seven Principles of Creative Leverage:
  - *always start from scratch;*
  - *demand a ruthlessly simple definition of the business problem;*
  - *discover a proprietary emotion;*
  - *focus on the size of the idea, not the size of the budget;*
  - *seek out strategic risks;*
  - *collaborate or perish;*
  - *listen hard to your customers (then listen some more).*

WHAT'S GOOD ABOUT IT

- Starting from scratch is harder said than done, and more marketers should do it, or at least investigate doing it.
- The principles at the heart of the book will resonate with anyone involved in any form of creative marketing:
  - ☐ creativity will be an increasingly essential business tool;
  - ☐ you can't buy creativity, but you can unlock it;
  - ☐ creativity is not an easy path to walk but the rewards are worth it.
- There are some good case histories from Skoda, Citibank, United Airlines and Lee Jeans.

WHAT YOU HAVE TO WATCH

- The authors are the founders of Fallon so at times the book can read like an agency brochure.
- The seven principles aren't that original or earth-shattering – a helpful reminder of good practice, but not stunningly new in any particular sense.
- American case histories such as Holiday Inn, EDS, and Bahamas Ministry of Tourism may be of less interest to UK readers.

Lovemarks KEVIN ROBERTS

WHAT THE BOOK SAYS

- The idealism of love is the new realism of business. By building respect and inspiring love, business can move the world.
- Once there were products, then trademarks, then brands and now lovemarks.
- For great brands to survive, they must create 'loyalty beyond reason'.
- The secret is to use mystery, sensuality and intimacy.
- Consumers, not companies, own lovemarks.
- Some truths about love: humans need it; it means more than liking a lot; it is about responding, about delicate

intuitive sensing; it takes time and it cannot be commanded or demanded.

- A picture may be worth a thousand words, but terrific stories are right up there with them. A great story can never be told too often.
- Great ideas, like humour, come from the corners of the mind, out on the edge. That's why humour can break up log-jams in business and personal relationships.

WHAT'S GOOD ABOUT IT

- The book is attempting to redefine brand thinking, and is thought-provoking.
- The warning signs of brands descending into generic stuff are: consistent, interchangeable, impersonal, abundant, homogenous and lowest price.
- 'Brands are out of juice' is an interesting notion: worn out from overuse; no longer mysterious; can't understand the new consumer; struggle with good old-fashioned competition; have been captured by formula; have been smothered by creeping conservatism.
- Human beings are powered by emotion, not by reason. The essential difference between emotion and reason is that emotion leads to action while reason leads to conclusions.
- Primary emotions: joy, sorrow, anger, fear, surprise and disgust can be outstripped by more complex secondary emotions: love, guilt, shame, pride, envy and jealousy.

WHAT YOU HAVE TO WATCH

- The action points at the end are all pretty hackneyed stuff: be passionate, involve customers, celebrate loyalty, find, tell and retell great stories, accept responsibility.
- Pretty much all the examples are from Saatchi clients, and at times it just sounds like a self-trumpeting agency brochure.

Manage your Reputation   ROGER HAYWOOD

WHAT THE BOOK SAYS

- It tells clients and people in PR agencies how to plan public relations to build and protect the organisation's most powerful asset – its reputation.
- It outlines the basic principles of PR, how the direction must be set from the top, and how to design and measure every type of programme.
- It argues that the attitude of someone taking a decision can be more important than the logical elements.
- A spontaneous reaction to your company or brand (the 'Pub Test') can be a decent measure of public relations.
- The best corporate behaviour is likely to be the most profitable.

WHAT'S GOOD ABOUT IT

- Asserting that company or brand reputation is everyone's responsibility might enable you to start deeper strategic conversations with your clients.
- Every practitioner's element to plan a good PR programme is here: developing the brief, writing the plan and measurement. There are whole chapters on public affairs, corporate and investor relations, issues and crisis planning.
- There is a section on how to develop an effective PR structure which summarises the thinking of all the industry bodies.
- There is also one on how clients should choose agencies, which should certainly be read as a reminder before any pitch or re-pitch.
- A number of the sub-heads can easily be extracted as good material for presentations. For example: *Choose your words carefully, Understand the other point of view, Encourage advice you do not want to hear, You learn nothing when you are talking* and *Consider the journalist's point of view*.

- There is a good distinction drawn between an aim (a direction in which progress is to be made) and an objective (a specific point to be reached).

WHAT YOU HAVE TO WATCH

- Compared to most modern books it is a bit dry, so you are best off lifting out the chunks that suit your particular needs, rather than reading it end to end.
- There is no revolutionary thinking here – it is more like a textbook of good practice.
- Most of it is more relevant to corporate PR than it is to consumer, technology or healthcare brands, so care needs to be taken when applying the thinking.

Marketing Judo   BARNES & RICHARDSON

WHAT THE BOOK SAYS

- You don't need a big budget to build a brand.
- The principles of judo, where brains matter more than brawn, can help (*Ju* means flexible and *Do* means way).
- The authors rejuvenated the Harry Ramsden's brand and now run their own company called *Marketing Judo*.
- The seven stages they propose are:
  - □ Getting the basics right (don't spend on marketing till the basics are working)
  - □ Picking the right partner (staff, advisors, celebrities, other brands)
  - □ Choosing the right opponent (sloths, not Geesinks)*
  - □ Getting the crowd on your side (creating your own fan club)
  - □ Using your size to your advantage (keeping fit, moving fast, staying focused)

*Anton Geesink was a 6' 6" judo player who beat everyone in the 1964 Olympics and forced the introduction of weight classification for the first time.

☐ Doing the unexpected (the competitive advantage of unpredictability)

☐ Keeping your balance (the benefits of planning for the unexpected)

WHAT'S GOOD ABOUT IT

- The point about choosing your competition is well made: spotting corporate sloths is a good way to identify competition you can beat.
- There are examples of those who get it right: Pret A Manger, Kettle Foods, Cobra Beer, Eddie Stobart (and Walkers as a Geesink).
- Having a Brains Day not a Budget Day is a good way of leading a brainstorm.
- The book is short and pithy.
- The method can be followed simply and used with clients.

WHAT YOU HAVE TO WATCH

- The orientation is all about what to do when you have no budget. This could be counter-productive with clients if handled insensitively.
- The majority of the examples are retail-based.
- The judo analogy is pushed a bit far in certain places.

Marketing Stripped Bare PATRICK FORSYTH

WHAT THE BOOK SAYS

- It claims to be an insider's guide to the secret rules of marketing.
- It covers everything from advertising and PR through to sales, distribution, CRM and electronic media.
- It claims that marketing is central to every company, but it doesn't have to be wrapped up in complicated jargon so that everyone gets confused.

WHAT'S GOOD ABOUT IT

- Although the content is quite simplistic if taken literally, it is written in a very amusing way so that it shouldn't offend anyone.

- As such it could be perfect to give as an educational tool to junior clients who think they know it all but don't.
- It gives you easy ways to write marketing plans, examine the promotional mix and organise research methodology, even if you have never officially been trained in these areas.
- It is full of good quotes to help presentations to clients:
  - ☐ *Opportunities are usually disguised as hard work, so most people do not recognise them*
  - ☐ *Pessimists make poor planners*
  - ☐ *There is only one thing in the world worse than being talked about, and that is not being talked about*
  - ☐ *If you call a spade a spade, you won't last long in the advertising business*
  - ☐ *An idea that is not dangerous is unworthy of being called an idea at all*
  - ☐ *If at first an idea isn't totally absurd, there's no hope for it*
  - ☐ *My interest is in the future because I am going to spend the rest of my life there*

WHAT YOU HAVE TO WATCH
- There are no models or diagrams to steal, so you have to use some ingenuity and diligence to extract usable material from it.
- If you take anything too literally from the book, you may be accused of either being cynical, or too simplistic.

Meatball Sundae   SETH GODIN

WHAT THE BOOK SAYS
- It is subtitled *How New Marketing is Transforming the Business World (and how to thrive in it)*.
- A meatball sundae is something messy, disgusting and ineffective, the result of two perfectly good things that don't go together. Meatballs are basic staples – the stuff that used to be marketed quite well with TV and other

mass market techniques. The sundae topping is the new marketing, which looks appealing to traditional companies but is useless at selling meatballs. He outlines 14 trends in new marketing:

☐ direct communication between producers and consumers;
☐ amplification of the voice of the consumer and independent authorities;
☐ need for an authentic story as the number of sources increases;
☐ extremely short attention spans due to clutter;
☐ the Long Tail;
☐ outsourcing;
☐ google and the dicing of everything;
☐ infinite channels of communication;
☐ direct communication and commerce between consumers and consumers;
☐ the shifts in scarcity and abundance;
☐ the triumph of big ideas;
☐ the shift from 'how many' to 'who';
☐ the wealthy are like us;
☐ new gatekeepers, no gatekeepers.

WHAT'S GOOD ABOUT IT

- For a century, successful organisations were built around traditional marketing tactics. New media alternatives have ended the guaranteed effectiveness of TV, and often deliver very fast results at almost no cost. But it doesn't work for everyone and asking what this stuff can do for you is the wrong question. The right one is how can we change our business.
- Interruption as a media thought no longer works. Consumers regard it as SPAM and just hit delete or skip.
- The Long Tail demonstrates that in almost every single market 'other' is the leading brand. Domination by hit products is fading.

- The classic bell curve with volume in the mid price range has been replaced by an inverted one, where very cheap and expensive are the most fertile areas.
- Ideas that spread through groups of people are far more powerful than ideas delivered at an individual.

WHAT YOU HAVE TO WATCH
- Nothing.

Panicology BRISCOE & ALDERSEY-WILLIAMS

WHAT THE BOOK SAYS
- It explains what is worth worrying about and what is not, based on true statistics rather than media hype.
- People in different countries fear different things (Danes about nuclear power, Italians about radiation from their mobile phones).
- Meanwhile, we all live longer and have better standards of living than ever.
- All the scare stories, including overpopulation, murder rates, fish shortages and obesity levels, are analysed and explained.
- We carry in our heads a bucket of worry that we seem compelled to fill with whatever is available.
- Many commercial interests add the spurious authority of a survey to support what they wish to say.
- We have a new IPOD generation: Insecure, Pressured, Over-taxed, Debt-ridden.
- A house buying multiple of 1:3 (average salary to house value) is 'affordable'. In London, this is over 1:6.

WHAT'S GOOD ABOUT IT
- You can see immediately the extraordinary extent to which statistics are manipulated and misrepresented by vested interests and the media.
- There is a sceptic's toolkit to help you work out whether something is valid or not: check for vested interest, weasel

words, surveys and who conducted them, percentages rather than actual numbers, and many other tricks.
* *'Mathematics is the quintessential way to make impressive-sounding claims which are devoid of factual content.'* John Allen Paulos.
* The cult of innumeracy means that most people can't tell what the truth is.
* You can look up any subject and get the correct facts, coupled with the sort of nonsense that much of the media build around the subject.

WHAT YOU HAVE TO WATCH
* Not much. It is well-written.
* The sections allow you to get any subject you want, but there is no sequence as such, so dipping would make it a lighter read.

Perfect Pitch   JON STEEL

WHAT THE BOOK SAYS
* Business presentations could and should be much better.
* It identifies a range of presentation crimes committed every day in business, and the pillars on which successful presentations are built.
* The importance of listening and understanding audience psychology is stressed.
* The rehearsal, the preparation, the leave-behind and the approach after the pitch are more important than the pitch itself.
* Don't lecture – communicate.
* Bullet points dilute thought, and clip art is a way of saying you have no imagination.
* The more connected we are, the less intelligent we become (the author ceremoniously runs over his BlackBerry with his Porsche, but it still works so he has to use his neighbour's sledgehammer to finish the job).

WHAT'S GOOD ABOUT IT
- There is a lot experience here in anecdote from 20 years in advertising.
- The pitch doesn't actually have to be perfect – just better than everyone else's.
- There is a five-step programme to be followed:
  - ☐ Grazing (data dump and gathering raw materials)
  - ☐ Looking for meaning (establish connections, write down all possible ideas)
  - ☐ Drop it (take a break, get away from the problem, view it afresh later)
  - ☐ Adapt and distil (make the ideas make sense to anybody, simplicity)
  - ☐ Writing the presentation
- There are lots of examples from politics and law as well as marketing (Churchill, the O.J. Simpson trial, London's 2012 Olympic bid).

WHAT YOU HAVE TO WATCH
- The book is heavy on anecdote, but not on method, so don't expect a step-by-step guide to how to run the perfect pitch.
- Most of the examples are American, so you need to be able to take the broad spirit of them and apply them in a UK context.

Quirkology RICHARD WISEMAN

WHAT THE BOOK SAYS
- Psychology and the quirky science of everyday life have a deep bearing on consumer behaviour and as such lie at the heart of business understanding.
- There is a reason for pretty much everything, so we are entitled to ask how our surnames influence our lives, why women should have men write their personal ads, and why people in Delhi are more helpful than Londoners.
- Findings include:

- ☐ Birth sign has no effect on behaviour at all, until people learn what their sign is and start behaving that way
- ☐ People can, within reason, choose when they die based on significant dates such as birthdays, and whether their inheritance will fall into a new tax year
- ☐ People can be made to remember things that they have never experienced
- ☐ The original idea of six degrees of separation has now gone down to four

WHAT'S GOOD ABOUT IT

- The author has conducted thousands of experiments that either challenge our preconceptions or provide new answers to age-old questions. These include:
  - ☐ People would rather wear a sweater that has been dropped in dog faeces and not washed, than one that has been dry-cleaned but used to belong to a mass murderer
  - ☐ The difference between a genuine and fake smile is all in the eyes – in a genuine smile, the skin around the eyes crinkles
  - ☐ The best way of detecting a lie is to listen, not look – liars say less, give fewer details and use the word 'I' less
  - ☐ Having a greater awareness of these possibilities could help all aspects of your life – business and social

WHAT YOU HAVE TO WATCH

- Although the book answers a lot of questions, it probably raises a lot more.
- It is intended to make the reader more interesting, but it could equally make you a trivia bore if not handled carefully.

Simply Brilliant   FERGUS O'CONNELL

WHAT THE BOOK SAYS
- The best ideas aren't always complicated and the incredibly straightforward stuff is often overlooked in the search for a complex answer.
- Many smart people lack the set of essential skills which could roughly be described as 'common sense'.
- There are seven principles here that can be adapted for attacking most everyday problems:
  - ☐ Many things are simple – *despite our tendency to complicate them*
  - ☐ You need to know what you're trying to do – *many don't*
  - ☐ There is always a sequence of events – *make the journey in your head*
  - ☐ Things don't get done if people don't do them – *strategic wafflers beware!*
  - ☐ Things rarely turn out as expected – *so plan for the unexpected*
  - ☐ Things either are or they aren't – *don't fudge things*
  - ☐ Look at things from others' point of view – *it will help your expectations*

WHAT'S GOOD ABOUT IT
- In a world of over-complication, asking some simple questions can really make your life easier. For example:
  - ☐ What would be the simplest thing to do here?
  - ☐ Describing an issue or a solution in less than 25 words
  - ☐ Telling it as though you were telling a six year old
  - ☐ Asking whether there is a simpler way
- Try writing the minutes of a meeting before the meeting – then you'll know what you want to get out of it.
- It highlights the difference between duration and effort. *'How long will it take you to have a look at that?' 'About an hour.'* But when?
- It explains the reasons why things don't get done: confusion, over-commitment, inability – usually busy people never say there's a problem!

- Plan your time assuming you will have interruptions – the *'hot date'* scenario.

WHAT YOU HAVE TO WATCH

- The orientation is very much based on a project management perspective, which is fine if you are one, but others may prefer to cherry-pick the most applicable ideas.
- Anyone who flies by the seat of their pants would have to be very disciplined to apply these ideas. It's a bit like dieting.

The Art of Creative Thinking JOHN ADAIR

WHAT THE BOOK SAYS

- Once you understand the creative process, you can train yourself to listen, look and read with a creative attitude. Techniques include:
  - ☐ Using the stepping stones of analogy (use normal things to suggest new uses)
  - ☐ Making the strange familiar and the familiar strange (analyse what you don't know about something you know well)
  - ☐ Widening your span of relevance (many inventions were conceived by those working in other fields)
  - ☐ Being constantly curious
  - ☐ Practising serendipity (the more you think, the more it appears you are in 'the right place at the right time')
  - ☐ Making better use of your Depth Mind (trust your sub-conscious to sort things out and generate solutions once you have 'briefed it')
  - ☐ Learning to tolerate ambiguity
  - ☐ Suspending judgement
  - ☐ Not waiting for inspiration – you have to make it happen

WHAT'S GOOD ABOUT IT

- This rather brilliant short book was originally written in 1990, so it is not riddled with modern jargon or method. It just tells it straight.
- Chance favours the prepared mind. By keeping your eyes open, listening for ideas and keeping a notebook, you can capture stimuli as they occur.
- It is full of inspirational comments from artists, scientists and philosophers:
- *'I invent nothing; I rediscover.'* Rodin
- *'Everything has been thought of before, but the problem is to think of it again.'* Goethe
- *'Discovery consists of seeing what everyone has seen and thinking what nobody has thought.'* Anon

WHAT YOU HAVE TO WATCH

- Nothing. Everyone should read it for life use as well as just creative thinking in business.

The Brand Innovation Manifesto JOHN GRANT

WHAT THE BOOK SAYS

- The days of big image branding are over, and that includes the USP, brand essence and cultural trends research, none of which do the job any more.
- Brands should be seen as clusters of cultural ideas, many of which can be contributed by consumers and other brands as well as the brand owners.
- The main concept in the book is the 'brand molecule', a modular structure to which new ideas can be added regularly.
- He offers 32 types of brand idea that can be stolen or cross-pollinated to reinvigorate tired brands.

WHAT'S GOOD ABOUT IT

- The idea of establishing a *Cultural Logic* as the basis of a strategy is an interesting one – brand activities can be

broad-ranging as long as they have a well-considered central theme.
- Those stuck in a strategic rut could do worse than to try drawing up their own brand molecule, using any number of his 32 brand elements:
  - *New Traditions:* habit, spectacular, leadership, organisation
  - *Belief Systems:* cognitive, appreciation, faith, atlas
  - *Time:* regressive, now, nostalgia, calendar
  - *Herd instincts:* initiation, crowd, clan, craze
  - *Connecting:* co-authored, socialising, cooperative, localised
  - *Luxury:* concierge, plenty, exclusive, exotic
  - *Provocative:* erotic, cathartic, scandal, radical
  - *Control:* personalised, in-control, competition, grading
- It is also helpful to bear in mind that few strategies are truly original – there is no sin in looking at other markets for inspiration and trying to apply the same thinking to yours.

WHAT YOU HAVE TO WATCH
- The Brand Molecule idea could run out of shape if not carefully handled – a random set of thoughts drawn as though they are connected, when in truth they are not, will not help.
- Some of the praise trumpeting the originality of the book is a bit misleading – in truth it synthesises, rather than originates, many ideas.

The Cluetrain Manifesto   LEVINE, LOCKE, SEARLS & WEINBERGER

WHAT THE BOOK SAYS
- The 'cluetrain' is simply following a chain of conversations on the Web.

- It is the end of business as usual because these conversations have changed forever the way companies need to interact with their customers.
- In fact, markets (customers) are now usually more intelligent than companies because they can exchange information faster.
- Customers and employees are openly communicating so there are no secrets any more – one-way rhetoric from head office simply doesn't wash.
- Companies that choose to ignore this are missing a massive opportunity.
- There are 95 theses designed to ignite a debate.

WHAT'S GOOD ABOUT IT

- It is interesting to consider that the appeal of the Internet is not the technology but peoples' desire to tell stories and communicate generally.
- It must be true that an employee who tells the internal truth about a company can cause havoc, so companies need to know how to deal with it. There is an example of someone in Canada being overcharged for a car service – the chain ends when an employee of the dealership explains how they load prices.
- Communications never should be one-way, and this is a poignant reminder.
- The 95 theses can be read in five minutes and are a good source of controversial quotes.

WHAT YOU HAVE TO WATCH

- It is a series of essays and as such lacks coherence.
- It is 'magnificently overstated', according to one critic – 'brilliant and impossible at the same time'.
- Most companies won't enjoy hearing the contents so care is needed with regard to what can realistically be done.

The E-Myth Revisited   MICHAEL E. GERBER

WHAT THE BOOK SAYS
- Most small businesses don't work, and here's what to do about it.
- There are two big myths about people who start their own businesses:
  - □ most are entrepreneurs (they probably aren't);
  - □ an individual who understands the technical work of a business can successfully run a business that does that technical work (this assumption is usually wrong and can be fatal).
- The Fatal Assumption: *if you understand the technical work of a business, you understand a business that does that technical work.*
- In fact, those running businesses need to be part entrepreneur, part manager, part technician. If they can't, then they need others to perform these roles. The first thinks ahead and dreams, the second controls and restrains, the third gets the work done.
- Businesses move from infancy (the technician's phase), to adolescence (getting some help), beyond the comfort zone to maturity.

WHAT'S GOOD ABOUT IT
- The turn-key revolution is a way of looking at your business that makes you behave like McDonald's from the very start. You have to record every little element that makes your business different and turn these into a virtue that is worth paying for.
- *'Contrary to popular belief, my experience has shown me that the people who are exceptionally good in business aren't so because of what they know but because of their insatiable need to know more.'*
- The idea of an *Entrepreneurial Seizure* is a good one. One day you suddenly ask *Why am I doing this?* and start imagining your own business.

- The dilemma for many small business owners is that they don't own a business, they own a job, which essentially has no value.
- 'The difference between creativity and innovation is the difference between thinking about getting things done in the world and getting things done.'

WHAT YOU HAVE TO WATCH
- This is all about small businesses, not the generalities of big business.

The End of Advertising as We Know it   SERGIO ZYMAN

WHAT THE BOOK SAYS
- Traditional advertising doesn't work, and is nothing to do with the standard notion of 30-second commercials.
- Awareness doesn't sell, so there is no point in pursuing it in its own right.
- Advertising is everything – packaging, spokespeople, employee relations, etc.
- Loyalty is a perishable commodity – brands must change or die.
- Fish where the fish are – stop looking for new users all the time.

WHAT'S GOOD ABOUT IT
- It has six new versions of old rules:

OLD	NEW
1. Give people budgets to spend wisely	1. Give projects budgets, not people
2. Awareness is king and assume people get it	2. Awareness is irrelevant, so over-communicate
3. Promote from within, grow organically	3. Teach continuously, get regular transfusions
4. Expand for success	4. Maximise your existing assets
5. Get lots of data	5. Get relevant data
6. Marketing is an expense	6. Marketing is an investment

- It has some useful definitions of a brand:
  - □ *A container for a customer's complete experience with the product*
  - □ *A bundle of functional and emotional benefits, attributes, experiences, symbols*
  - □ *The company's links to the likes, wants and needs of its customers*
  - □ *What keeps a company's loyal users coming back*
- He makes good sense on crisis management:
  - □ *Have your response come from the top*
  - □ *Tell the truth, tell it all, and tell it fast*
  - □ *Do something to make it better*
  - □ *Have a theme and stick to the script*
  - □ *Know when to shut up*
  - □ *Keep your PR people in the loop*

WHAT YOU HAVE TO WATCH
- The author is the former Chief Marketing Officer of Coca-Cola so, although he thinks he knows it all, he probably doesn't.
- Implementing his approach might upset the balance of teamwork because he is so opinionated.

The End of Marketing as We Know it   SERGIO ZYMAN

WHAT THE BOOK SAYS
- Marketing today is all about image, but it isn't working properly.
- Marketing is a science, not an art.
- Marketing is too important to be left to the marketing department.
- Marketers must be accountable to shareholders.
- Focus on results, not activities.
- Megabrands are a rotten idea.

WHAT'S GOOD ABOUT IT

- It is full of ballsy assertions such as *Traditional marketing is not dying, it's dead, and Why have marketing? To make money.*
- The section on *How to sell the most stuff and make the most money* has some helpful steps you can copy:
  - ☐ *How to make positioning a two-way street*
  - ☐ *How branding creates identity*
  - ☐ *How to stop brands becoming static*
  - ☐ *How to compete against yourself*
  - ☐ *How to define consumer expectations that your competitors can't meet*
- All the quotes you want are in bold for easy picking:
  - ☐ 'When you start looking at exactly how much things cost and how much profit you are getting...you become a much better marketer'
  - ☐ 'Narrow how your competitor is defined to a single trait or quality whilst simultaneously broadening yours'
  - ☐ 'The old conventional thinking that said that if you grab people's hearts, their wallets will follow is dead, kaput, finished...people need reasons to buy'
- At the end there are the 28 principles of new marketing.

WHAT YOU HAVE TO WATCH

- The author is the former Chief Marketing Officer of Coca-Cola, so there are a lot of Coke examples.
- He has a bit of a chip on his shoulder about being disliked by creative ad agencies, which can make some of his points defensive ('Agencies can never make smart, fully informed decisions because they are never going to be fully informed').
- The 28 principles of new marketing aren't exactly new.
- Implementing his approach might encourage machismo in the office.

The Laws of Simplicity John Maeda

WHAT THE BOOK SAYS

* Simplicity = Sanity. There are ten laws of simplicity:
  1. *Reduce.* The simplest way to achieve simplicity is through thoughtful reduction.
  2. *Organise.* Organisation makes a system of many appear fewer.
  3. *Time.* Savings in time feel like simplicity.
  4. *Learn.* Knowledge makes everything simpler.
  5. *Differences.* Simplicity and complexity need each other.
  6. *Context.* What lies in the periphery of simplicity is definitely not peripheral.
  7. *Emotion.* More emotions are better than fewer.
  8. *Trust.* In simplicity we trust.
  9. *Failure.* Some things can never be made simple.
  10. *The One.* Simplicity is about subtracting the obvious, and adding the meaningful.

WHAT'S GOOD ABOUT IT

* The book is short, which it should be. It has a number of systems for reducing the complex down to simpler thinking. There are three keys:
  1. *Away.* More appears like less by simply moving it far away.
  2. *Open.* Openness simplifies complexity.
  3. *Power.* Use less, gain more.
* There are plenty of thought-provoking ideas to sort out complex things: *How simple can you make it? v. How complex does it have to be? How can you make the wait shorter? v. How can you make the wait more tolerable?*
* SHE: Shrink, Hide, Embody.
* SLIP: Sort, Label, Integrate, Prioritise.
* BRAIN: Basics, Repeat, Avoid (desperation), Inspire, Never (forget to repeat).

WHAT YOU HAVE TO WATCH
- The author has a preoccupation with technology, so many of the examples are tech-related.

The Long Tail   CHRIS ANDERSON

WHAT THE BOOK SAYS
- Endless choice is creating unlimited demand.
- Traditional business models suggest that high-selling hits are required for success. These are at the high-volume end of a conventional demand curve.
- But in the Internet era, the combined value of the millions of items that only sell in small quantities can equal or even exceed the best sellers.
- Modest sellers and niche products are now becoming an immensely powerful cumulative force. In this respect, many 'mass' markets are turning into millions of aggregated niches.

WHAT'S GOOD ABOUT IT
- This is a very original and thought-provoking book. It takes a while to get into, but it's worth it.
- It introduces reasonably complicated mathematical theory in a user-friendly way, particularly micro-analysis of the very end of a very long tail. This is where helpful truths about the economics of your market can be seen properly.
- Contemporary examples from music (radio and album sales), books and films lend a populist slant to the theory, which should appeal widely.
- Old theories such as the 80/20 rule receive a thorough going-over. It's never exactly 80/20, and the percentages can apply to different things (products, sales or profits). And they don't add up to 100.
- The nine big rules of the Long Tail are:
  1. Move inventory way in...or way out
  2. Let customers do the work
  3. One distribution method doesn't fit all

4. One product doesn't fit all
5. *One price doesn't fit all*
6. *Share information (lose control)*
7. *Think 'and', not 'or'*
8. *Trust the market to do your job*
9. *Understand the power of free*

WHAT YOU HAVE TO WATCH

* The model works best with true Internet and digital products that do not take up any storage space. For example, Amazon books still require storage space that has a cost. iTunes do not. So careful thought is required as to the nature of the market you are analysing.

The New Marketing Manifesto   JOHN GRANT

WHAT THE BOOK SAYS

* There are 12 rules of New Marketing:
  □ *Get up close and personal*: become intimate rather than public and formal
  □ *Tap basic human needs*: there are 15 fundamental human drives*
  □ *Author innovation*: brand identities should be fluid, not fixed
  □ *Mythologise the new*: don't just reflect the status quo – create possibilities
  □ *Create tangible differences in the experience*: sound, smell, touch, taste
  □ *Cultivate authenticity*: as opposed to false 'sincerity' (see *Affluenza*)
  □ *Work through consensus*: forget targeting, encircle and involve audiences
  □ *Open up to participation*: customers should be able to influence the brand
  □ *Build communities of interest*: don't classify them, let them belong

☐ *Use strategic creativity*: look at Why? How? Where? not standard media
☐ *Stake a claim to fame*: do something memorable; you can't buy fame
☐ *Follow a vision and be true to your values*: set the goal and pursue it

*They are sex, hunger, physicality, avoiding distress, curiosity, honour, order, vengeance, social contact, family, prestige, power, citizenship, independence and social acceptance.

• New Marketing is more creative; it treats brands as living ideas that can transform people; it is entrepreneurial, more humanist and less scientific; it favours constant change over conservatism; it is part of a new consumer culture.

WHAT'S GOOD ABOUT IT
• It is an easy read, well laid out with hundreds of examples.
• There are lots of case studies if you need markets to compare: IKEA, Tango, Pizza Express, French Connection, British Telecom, Egg and more.

WHAT YOU HAVE TO WATCH
• The book was written in 1999 so some of the ideas have moved on somewhat.

The Philosophy of Branding   THOM BRAUN

WHAT THE BOOK SAYS
• There are strong links between philosophy and branding (*'All modern, complex and apparently sophisticated approaches to brands and branding must be grounded in a rigorous and philosophical view of the way the world works'*).
• It works its way through the thinking of most of the major philosophers and expresses their views as though they were in charge of brands.

- It starts with Heraclitus, moving through Socrates, Plato, Aristotle, Descartes, Locke, Hume, Kant, Hegel, Nietzsche, Wittgenstein and Popper.
- It all comes together in a list of top tips which summarises their thinking as though they were applying it to brand management.

WHAT'S GOOD ABOUT IT

- This is certainly a highly original way of looking at brand management and should stimulate some new, more cerebral approaches.
- It is also an excellent way to acquaint yourself with the gist of most philosophical thinking, without reading the original impenetrable essays.
- The writing style is jargon-free and short, so you can read it quickly.
- It is fairly simple to apply the thinking, and back it up with intellectual stature, for example:
  - *Nothing is stable in the world*
  - *Question everything*
  - *'Irreducible' (certain) brand cores should be viewed against the constant process of it becoming something else*
  - *Don't be overly rational or logical*
  - *Don't be fooled into thinking you know everything about markets, consumers or your own brand*
  - *Pose a thesis, then the antithesis and arrive at a synthesis (the dialectic)*

WHAT YOU HAVE TO WATCH

- Perhaps not surprisingly, a lot of the theories are contradictory, so you cannot use them all together.
- Of course, none of the thinking here was ever applied to brands, so you have to check your relevance from time to time and keep a sense of perspective.

The Pirate Inside ADAM MORGAN

WHAT THE BOOK SAYS
- Powerful brands are built by people, not by proprietary methodologies.
- The real issue is not the strategy, but how we need to *behave* when an organisation's systems seem more geared to slowing and diluting, than spurring and galvanising.
- To achieve this you need to be a *Constructive Pirate*. This is not the same as anarchy where there are 'no rules', but it requires a different *set* of rules.
- It shows how to write your own 'Articles' in your organisation.
- Even in big organisations, you need challenger sub-cultures.

WHAT'S GOOD ABOUT IT
- It explains nine ways of behaving that stimulate challenger brand cultures:
  1. *Outlooking*: looking for different kinds of insights by:
     - *Emotional Insertion* – Putting a new kind of emotion into the category
     - *Overlay* – Overlaying the rules of a different category onto your own
     - *Brand Neighbourhoods* – Radically re-framing your competitive set
     - *Grip* – Finding a place for the brand to gain traction in contemporary culture
  2. *Pushing* – Pushing ideas well beyond the norm
  3. *Projecting* – Being consistent across far more media than the usual
  4. *Wrapping* – Communicating less conventionally with customers
  5. *Denting* – Respecting colleagues whilst making a real difference
  6. *Binding* – Having a contract that ensures everyone comes with the idea
  7. *Leaning* – Pushing harder for sustained commitment
  8. *Refusing* – Having the passion to say no

9. *Taking it personally* – A different professionalism that transcends corporate man
- *Biting the Other Generals* is a good concept based on an anecdote from the Seven Years War. A brilliantly unconventional General, James Wolfe, proved himself one of the most talented military leaders under King George III. When some of Wolfe's detractors tried to undermine him by complaining that he was mad, the king replied: 'Oh, he is mad, is he? Then I would he would bite some other of my generals'.
- *The Three Buckets* is a good exercise whereby clients have to categorise all their existing projects into *Brilliant Basics*, *Compelling Differences* and *Changing the Game* – usually with poignant results.

WHAT YOU HAVE TO WATCH
- Not much. This is an excellent book and you can use the exercises with pretty much any business.

The Play Ethic   PAT KANE

WHAT THE BOOK SAYS
- Politicians arguing consistently for a work ethic are missing the point. We are essentially designed to play.
- We all think we know what play is (what we do as children, outside work, and for no other reason than pleasure), but understanding the real meaning of it would revolutionise and liberate our daily lives.
- Huge numbers of companies now make their money out of play elements – who is to say that is wrong? Play offers learning, progress, imagination, a sense of self, identity and contest. It is also the fermenting ground for exploring alternatives – the essence of creativity.
- Your mind is a 'possibility factory' – use it.
- The new generation of Soulitarians is more interested in the quality of life and what they do for a living than the money. They are Lifestyle Militants.

- Poiesis is the act of producing something specified – too few people can do this.

WHAT'S GOOD ABOUT IT
- The idea that when work becomes too humane (nice to do), we do too much of it is interesting.
- Sick-related stress costs companies £370m a year – they should be more enlightened about job sharing and working from home.
- Much so-called play (such as computer games) constitute 'hard fun' – if they do not represent a challenge, they aren't considered to be good.
- '*I think, therefore I produce*' is an interesting new credo for people in the information age.
- Technology was supposed to make our lives easier, but it annihilates our time by intruding on every moment of the day – we need to offset this.

WHAT YOU HAVE TO WATCH
- This is a complicated and detailed read. You could dip in, but it is more of a long essay or dissertation, so it is best to read end to end.
- It is very widely researched, but you would have to work extra hard to track down all the lines of enquiry that it suggests.

The Tipping Point   MALCOLM GLADWELL

WHAT THE BOOK SAYS
- Little things can make a big difference.
- Explains and defines the 'tipping point' – the moment at which ideas, trends and social behaviour cross a threshold, tip and spread like wildfire.
- Just as one sick person can start an epidemic, very minor adjustments to products or ideas can make them far more likely to be a success.
- The overall message of the book is that, contrary to the belief that big results require big efforts that are beyond

the capacity of the single individual, one imaginative person applying a well-placed lever can move the world.

WHAT'S GOOD ABOUT IT

- It is optimistic in outlook and suggests that individuals can make a significant contribution. It cites the example of Paul Revere who, in 1775, overheard a conversation and rode all night to warn Americans in Boston that the British would attack in the morning. The Americans were ready and defeated them.
- The following three areas are a good working template for all communications:
  1. *The Law of the Few* – the idea that the nature of the messenger is critical
  2. *The Stickiness Factor* – the quality of the message has to be good enough to be worth acting on
  3. *The Power of Context* – people are exquisitely sensitive to changes of time, place and circumstance

WHAT YOU HAVE TO WATCH

- The three areas aren't that original – they are roughly similar to medium, message and target audience.
- It is easy to get distracted by the three groups of people who may start a tipping point: *Connectors* (people who know a lot of people), *Mavens* (those who accumulate knowledge, but are not persuaders), and *Salesmen* (people who are very persuasive). These may be more relevant to PR than paid-for communication.
- It is quite American, with many examples relating to the US (for example, how removing graffiti reduced the crime rate in New York in the eighties). Thought is needed with regard to application elsewhere.
- Even if a marketing strategy overtly sets out to create a tipping point, it is so idiosyncratic and hard to predict that it might not work.

The Wisdom of Crowds   James Surowiecki

WHAT THE BOOK SAYS

- The book is subtitled *Why the Many are Smarter than the Few* and was first aired by the author as a column in *The New Yorker* magazine.
- History tells us that when you want something done you turn to a leader: right? Wrong. If you want to make a correct decision or solve a problem, large groups of people are smarter than a few experts.
- The theory of the wisdom of crowds has huge implications for the way we run our businesses, structure our political systems, and organise our society.
- When Charles Mackay wrote in 1841 about *Extraordinary Popular Decisions* and the *Madness of Crowds*, he presented an endlessly entertaining chronicle of mass manias and collective follies. This book proposes the opposite.

WHAT'S GOOD ABOUT IT

- The book could change the way you think about human behaviour. His points include:
  - □ In 1906 800 people guessed the weight of an ox. Their average was exactly right.
  - □ In 1968 a submarine was lost, and only when several scenarios were pieced together did they find it.
  - □ On *Who wants to be a millionaire?* the experts (phone a friend) are right 61 per cent of the time, and the crowd 91 per cent
- *The difference difference makes*: tiny changes can make for mass acceptance.
- *Monkey see, monkey do*: independence is important to intelligent decision making.
- *Putting the pieces together*: decentralisation (letting go) makes for better collective decisions.
- *Shall we dance?* Coordination is possible in a complex world, as evidenced by how huge numbers of people successfully navigate their way round busy city streets.

- *Committees, juries and teams*: these do not make good decisions if they are led in a certain direction by the chairperson.
- *The company*: meet the new boss, same as the old boss? Companies that coordinate their behaviour with that of their customers do better, such as Zara delivering new lines twice a week instead of once a fashion season.

WHAT YOU HAVE TO WATCH
- There are no clear sections so you have to burrow deep for these nuggets.

The 22 Irrefutable Laws of Advertising
MICHAEL NEWMAN

WHAT THE BOOK SAYS
- The full title is *The 22 Irrefutable Laws of Advertising (and When to Violate them)* – a series of essays by the great and the good including Dave Trott, Kevin Roberts, James Lowther, and MT Rainey.
- There is one essay on each law, most of which are self-explanatory: Simplicity, Positioning, Consistency, Selling, Emotion, Love, Experience, Relevance, Humour, Disruption, Jump, Fascination, Irreverence, Taste, Topicality, Chat, Nice, Negativity, Execution, Evolution.
- Those that need explanation are: The Silver Elephant (the intent to produce something that has never been done before, and the act of carrying it out), and The Outlaw (everything we have told you is a lie, including this).

WHAT'S GOOD ABOUT IT
- There are lots of different opinions here, so you are not reading 200 pages all making the same point.
- At the end there is a list of crimes against advertising: research, logic, familiarity, self-importance, humanity (cheesiness), atheism (lack of opinion), strangulation by data, interference, pitching for free, and commoditisation of the creative product.

- The author sets up a decent introduction grappling with the tricky business of how to catch lightning in a bottle (the elusive search for genuine creativity), and 'how bad is it, doc?' (a quick rundown on the problems currently facing the advertising industry).
- Anyone experiencing a blockage in their communications should be able to dip into one of the theories and pull out a new approach to their issue.
- Dave Trott's binary brief is particularly useful – the brief is constructed simply by choosing one of only two alternatives to each of the normal questions you would expect to address in a creative brief (not multiple options).

WHAT YOU HAVE TO WATCH
- There is no coherent message, so don't look for one.
- The author's comments on the contributors verge on the sycophantic.
- The book is a bit schizophrenic about whether all the laws should be obeyed, or ignored – you choose!

Welcome to the Creative Age MARK EARLS

WHAT THE BOOK SAYS
- Old-fashioned marketing is dead. It used to be about selling more than the other guy, but now it is mistakenly embraced as an organisational philosophy.
- Creativity is our greatest gift, but we don't always use it effectively.
- Four big things have changed the face of marketing:
  1. There is too much of everything (every market is over-supplied)
  2. The end of the consumer (people are confident and understand what marketing people are doing)
  3. The rise of the consumer as activist
  4. The demanding employee (the company man is dead)

WHAT'S GOOD ABOUT IT

- *Creative Age Ideas*; assume that audiences are neither listening nor interested; don't try to fit in (in fact usually challenge) and are often the result of strongly held beliefs, not rational analysis.
- These are re-named *'Purpose Ideas'*: what counts is what you want to change about the world (what is your purpose?).
- The 'added-value banana' anecdote, in which one is packaged as a 'fresh banana snack' ideal to be eaten on the move (all of which we know already), is salutary about the insanity of much modern marketing.
- The book tells you how to have ideas like this by identifying your purpose (not your positioning) and deciding on interventions (it's what you *do* that counts).
- There are lots of good mantras such as 'leave your agenda at the door', 'the brand ties you to the past', 'benchmarking yourself into a corner' and 'control is an illusion we are better off without'.
- There are whole chapters on why advertising people don't know how advertising works, and how to put *Purpose Ideas* at the heart of a business.

WHAT YOU HAVE TO WATCH

- Depending on what you do for a living, some of this might be unsettling and make the opposite of the case you desire, for example *'Fact: most of the people in an ad agency are not paid to be inventive or creative but to manage and service the ad-factory machinery'*.
- Any book that declares the death of something has to propose new ways forward. This one only half does, by setting you thinking for yourself.

We-Think   CHARLES LEADBEATER

WHAT THE BOOK SAYS

- The future is us, via mass collaboration, not mass production.
- The rallying call of the Web is for shared power that makes society more open and egalitarian.
- There has been an unparalleled wave of democratic, productive and creative participation online. This book is itself an example.
- The generation growing up with the Web will not be content to remain spectators. They want to be players and their slogan is '*We think therefore we are.*'
- Self-determination is a powerful thing. In 1998, BT had failed to get its field engineers to work harder so set up a *Freedom to Choose* scheme whereby they scheduled their own work. After three years they were working two hours a week less and earning more. Productivity was up five per cent and quality was up eight per cent.

WHAT'S GOOD ABOUT IT

- *You are what you share* is the new mantra, and the author works through numerous examples of how this works in the modern world, all facilitated by the Web.
- The roots of we-think reside in a strange mixture of online contributors:
  - □ *The academic* who brings a belief that knowledge develops through sharing ideas and testing them through peer review
  - □ *The hippie* who brings a deep scepticism about all sources of authority
  - □ *The peasant* who favours shared use of communal facilities and resources
  - □ *The geek* who offers to realise their dreams by networking them together
- When you put all this together, you have a powerful blend.

- The way it works is to start with the *core*, then other people *contribute* to it, they *connect* over it, they *collaborate* and they *create*. These are the Five Cs.

WHAT YOU HAVE TO WATCH

- It is not set out in any particular sections. It is more like a very long essay. As such it is not easy to dip in and out, or to refer back to something in particular. So it is best to treat it as a thought-provoking whole, rather than anything specific you can take action on.

Online resources

Eating the Big Fish, Adam Morgan:
www.eatbigfish.com

The Pirate Inside, Adam Morgan:
www.eatbigfish.com

The Long Tail, Chris Anderson:
www.thelongtail.com

Flat Earth News, Nick Davies:
www.flatearthnews.net

In Search of the Obvious, Jack Trout:
www.troutandpartners.com

The End of Marketing as We Know It, Sergio Zyman:
www.zyman.com

Meatball Sundae, Seth Godin:
www.sethgodin.com

The End of Advertising as We Know It, Sergio Zyman:
www.zyman.com

The Cluetrain Manifesto, Levine, Locke, Searls, and
    Weinberger:
www.cluetrain.com

Lovemarks, Kevin Roberts:
www.lovemarks.com

Quirkology, Richard Wiseman:
www.quirkology.com

Panicology, Briscoe & Aldersey-Williams:
www.panicology.com

Affluenza, Oliver James:
www.selfishcapitalist.com

Herd, Mark Earls:
www.herd.typepad.com

The Wisdom of Crowds, James Surowiecki:
www.randomhouse.com/features/wisdomofcrowds

Blink, Malcolm Gladwell:
www.gladwell.com/blink/index.html

The Tipping Point, Malcolm Galdwell:
www.gladwell.com/tippingpoint/index.html

The Play Ethic, Pat Kane:
www.theplayethic.com

Welcome to the Creative Age, Mark Earls:
www.herd.typepad.com

Juicing the Orange, Fallon & Senn:
www.juicingtheorange.com

Marketing Judo, Barns & Richardson:
www.marketingjudo.co.uk/

The Art of Creative Thinking, John Adair:
www.johnadair.co.uk/published.html

We-Think, Charles Leadbeater:
www.wethinkthebook.net

The Laws of Simplicity, John Maeda:
www.lawsofsimplicity.com

BIBLIOGRAPHY

CHAPTER 1

Hofmeyr, Jan and Butch Rice. *Commitment-led Marketing*. London: John Wiley, 2000.

Morgan, Adam. *Eating the Big Fish*. London: John Wiley, 1999.

Davies, Nick. *Flat Earth News*. London: Vintage, 2008.

Trout, Jack. *In Search of the Obvious*. London: John Wiley, 2008.

Anderson, Chris. *The Long Tail*. London: Random House, 2006.

Morgan, Adam. *The Pirate Inside*. London: John Wiley, 2004.

Updegraff, Robert R. *Obvious Adams: The Story of a Successful Business Man*. Louisville, KY: Updegraff Press, 1953

CHAPTER 2

Forsyth, Patrick. *Marketing Stripped Bare*. London: Kogan Page, 1990.

Godin, Seth. *Meatball Sundae*. London: Piatkus, 2007.

Levine, Rick, Christopher Locke, Doc Searls and David Weinberger. *The Cluetrain Manifesto*. London: Pearson, 2000.

Zyman, Sergio. *The End of Advertising as We Know it*. London: John Wiley, 2002.

Zyman, Sergio. *The End of Marketing as We Know it*. London: Harper Collins, 1999.

Grant, John. *The New Marketing Manifesto*. London: Orion, 1999.

CHAPTER 3

Pringle, Hamish and William Gordon. *Brand Manners*. London: John Wiley, 2001.

Salzman, Marian, Ira Matathia and Ann O'Reilly. *Buzz*. London: John Wiley, 2003.

Robert, Kevin. *Lovemarks*. New York: Powerhouse, 2004.

Haywood, Roger. *Manage your Reputation*. London: Kogan Page, 1994.

Grant, John. *The Brand Innovation Manifesto*. London: John Wiley, 2006.

Braun, Thom. *The Philosophy of Branding*. London: Kogan Page, 2004.

CHAPTER 4

James, Oliver. *Affluenza*. London: Random House, 2007.

Gladwell, Malcolm. *Blink*. London: Allen Lane, 2005.

Naish, John. *Enough*. London: Hodder & Stoughton, 2008.

Earls, Mark. *Herd*. London: John Wiley, 2007.

Briscoe, Simon and Hugh Aldersey-Williams. *Panicology*. London: Viking, 2008.

Wiseman, Richard. *Quirkology*. London: Pan Macmillan, 2007.

Gladwell, Malcolm. *The Tipping Point*. London: Little, Brown, 2000.

Surowiecki, James. *The Wisdom of Crowds*. London: Abacus, 2004.

CHAPTER 5

Pease, Allan and Wayne Lotherington. *Flicking your Creative Switch*. London: John Wiley, 2003.

Fellon, Pat and Fred Senn. *Juicing the Orange*. Boston: Harvard Business School Press, 2006.

Barnes, John and Richard Richardson. *Marketing Judo.*
London: Pearson, 2003.
Newman, Michael. *The 22 Irrefutable Laws of Advertising.*
London: John Wiley, 2004.
Adair, John. *The Art of Creative Thinking.* London: Kogan
Page, 1990.
Kane, Pat. *The Play Ethic.* London: Pan, 2004.
Earls, Mark. *Welcome to the Creative Age.* London: John
Wiley, 2002.
Leadbeater, Charles. *We-Think.* London: Profile, 2008.

CHAPTER 6

Heller, Richard. *High Impact Speeches.* London: Pearson,
2003.
Kean, David. *How Not to Come Second.* London: Cyan, 2006.
Steel, John. *Perfect Pitch.* London: John Wiley, 2007.
O'Connell, Fergus. *Simply Brilliant.* London: Pearson, 2001.
Gerber, Michael E. *The E-Myth Revisited.* London: Harper
Business, 1995.
Maeda, John. *The Laws of Simplicity.* Massachusettes: MIT
Press, 2006.

Also by the author

Business Greatest Hits. London: A&C Black, 2010.
Run Your Own Business. London: Hodder & Stoughton,
2010.
Small Business Survival. London; Hodder & Stoughton,
2010.
So What? London: Capstone, 2008.
Start. London: Capstone, 2008.
Tick Achieve. London: Capstone, 2008.

Index